T0328599

Cambridge Elements

Elements in Women Theatre Makers
edited by
Elaine Aston
Lancaster University
Melissa Sihra
Trinity College Dublin

MAYA RAO AND INDIAN FEMINIST THEATRE

Bishnupriya Dutt
Jawaharlal Nehru University

CAMBRIDGE
UNIVERSITY PRESS

CAMBRIDGE
UNIVERSITY PRESS

University Printing House, Cambridge CB2 8BS, United Kingdom

One Liberty Plaza, 20th Floor, New York, NY 10006, USA

477 Williamstown Road, Port Melbourne, VIC 3207, Australia

314–321, 3rd Floor, Plot 3, Splendor Forum, Jasola District Centre,
New Delhi – 110025, India

103 Penang Road, #05–06/07, Visioncrest Commercial, Singapore 238467

Cambridge University Press is part of the University of Cambridge.

It furthers the University's mission by disseminating knowledge in the pursuit of
education, learning, and research at the highest international levels of excellence.

www.cambridge.org
Information on this title: www.cambridge.org/9781009073172
DOI: 10.1017/9781009071987

First published 2022

A catalogue record for this publication is available from the British Library.

ISBN 978-1-009-07317-2 Paperback
ISSN 2634-2391 (online)
ISSN 2634-2383 (print)

Maya Rao and Indian Feminist Theatre

Elements in Women Theatre Makers

DOI: 10.1017/9781009071987
First published online: August 2022

Bishnupriya Dutt
Jawaharlal Nehru University
Author for correspondence: Bishnupriya Dutt, bishnupriyapaul@gmail.com

Abstract: Maya Rao, performer, performance maker, and feminist, has not only contributed to Indian feminist theatre but is also a trailblazer who set new standards in solo performances, mapped an alternate career trajectory for women in theatre, and, in the face of right-wing state repression in India, has engaged significantly in performance activism. This Element looks back at her early career in the 1980s, when she was creating agitprop theatre for the feminist movement, and forward to her performance activism in the twenty-first century, with detailed attention to Rao's acclaimed protest *Walk* and her participation in the protests against the Citizenship Amendment Act. The study also encompasses her parallel work in the theatre, from early collaborations with feminist directors to her solo projects. The author traces her creative-political journey towards an egalitarian feminist future.

Keywords: Maya Krishna Rao, performance activism, gender, experimental theatre, solo performances

ISBNs: 9781009073172 (PB), 9781009071987 (OC)
ISSNs: 2634-2391 (online), 2634-2383 (print)

Contents

1 Introduction

In *Lady Macbeth Revisited* (2008) and *Are You Home Lady Macbeth?* (2010), only a semblance of Shakespeare's tragedy remains. The Bard has a long history in India, but rarely has his work been subjected to such a radical intervention – more specifically a trenchant feminist intervention on the part of performance maker and activist Maya Krishna Rao.

Reducing the text to mere citations and deploying multimedia effects, Rao plays Lady Macbeth like a witch; going by her appearance and costume, she could be either. Instead of the tragic, Rao mobilizes the grotesque: enlarged images of her face (painstakingly painted) (Figure 1), unruly mass of white hair, or hands and feet are digitally projected, made monstrous, on a screen. This witch/ Lady Macbeth is displaced or dislocated but highly domesticated. Her household chores include ironing, cooking, preparing for the banquet, laying out crockery and cutlery on a long mat in an oriental style of hospitality, and sweeping the floor. And yet this routine domestic labour transforms into ritual-istic dances and chants reminiscent of witches; she may sweep the mat laid out for the banquet, but she also splashes it with blood (Figure 2) and plays hopscotch on the blood-spattered pattern. Confined to the house, the witch/ Lady Macbeth plots murders and devises power games, but she also plays cards with the devil and creates toys and voodoo bridal dolls. As Rao says, 'She is caught in a vortex, because she is out of joint with herself. We tread a thin line – is it real or is it play?' (Rao, 2021a).

I open with this snapshot of Rao's radical reinterpretation of *Macbeth* to introduce her dissent from the reverence for and conventional staging of canonical plays and signature style of performance in which the body is core to creating countercultural sites of feminist resistance. Now in her late sixties, Rao has been performing for more than forty years. Her career dates back to the late 1970s, when she was creating agitprop theatre with and for the feminist movement. This involved performing in the streets and in theatre venues, as well as appearing on makeshift stages – in college and school auditoriums and halls, studio spaces, art galleries, or in site-specific contexts. Postcolonial debates on theatre, regarded as an import of colonial cultural practice, often posit a binary between the theatre and the streets, arguing that theatre constitutes what Lara Shalson, quoting Christopher Balme, cites as the 'theatrical public sphere' that is outside the real public sphere and governed by its own conven-tions, so much so that it 'has become to all intent and purpose a private space' (quoted in Shalson, 2017: 23). Hence, theatre has come to be regarded as exclusive and accessible only to the urban middle classes. Contrastingly, street theatre, particularly in India, is seen as connected to the public sphere; many

Figure 1 *Lady Macbeth Revisited*: Maya Rao as Lady Macbeth and the witch
(Photo by Thyagarajan/National School of Drama archives)

Figure 2 *Lady Macbeth Revisited*: Maya Rao sweeping blood on the mat (Photo
by Thyagarajan/National School of Drama archives)

artists view the street as important to making a political statement through their
work. That said, Rao's binary crossings between the theatre and the streets have
proved vital to achieving a significant dialogue between the two. To public

spaces she brings the radical, experimental, feminist edge of her theatre work; her solo shows, destined for the theatre, incorporate long episodes from her street theatre. Both are explored in this study, as I trace and assess not only the impact of her performance activism, but also her contribution to feminist theatre practices in India.

My analysis is guided by three key questions. Firstly, how are we to historicize and contextualize the role of feminist-theatre activism as part of the broader public strategies and mobilization of women's movements in India? Secondly, with the decline of organized feminist and other social movements, what role can feminist performance activism play, especially in the context of a right-wing state unashamedly propagating patriarchy? And, thirdly, in what ways can the significant body of work generated by women in Indian theatre be identified as a feminist theatre practice? All three questions are prompted by Rao, a feminist theatre maker committed to contesting inequalities and injustices in India. Her creative-political journey has been long and arduous. It has been especially demanding due to the rise of neoliberalism that, in a country like India with high levels of poverty, adversely impacted economically and socially vulnerable communities, and because of the nation's swing to the draconian right in recent years. In brief, the political path Rao navigates as a feminist theatre maker is, like that of her witchlike Lady Macbeth, a bloodied one.

2 Women on the Streets: The Feminist Movement and Agitprop Theatre

An auction is about to begin and the vendor has a double task – to start the play by settling the audience down on the ground and to shout out the qualities of the wares he is exhibiting: grooms ready for marriage. Prospective grooms are carried in on the shoulders of other actors while the vendor tries to raise the price as much as possible in terms of a dowry:[1]

> Vendor: 'Marriage, marriage – now everyone's daughters and sisters can expect to find suitable grooms – a wide variety of choices – many kinds of grooms – one for everybody – everyone will get one; IAS, bankers, businessman, doctor, engineer, teacher, every-type – every-kind – one for everyone – everybody can now get one. (*Om Swaha*, 1988: 43)

One after the other, the coveted prospective grooms are brought in, but the choice of the buyer – the bride's father or brother – is determined by the price he can afford to pay. Even after the initial transaction has been settled prior to the

---

[1] Dowry is a widely prevalent practice in India, where marriages are arranged and the bride's family pays, in cash and gifts, a hefty sum to the groom's household. It exacerbates the notion of women as a transaction.

marriage, the financial demand does not cease, reflecting a common reality in dowry cases. When the bride's family cannot or are reluctant to pay more, so begins a period of mental and physical torture for the woman who is now living with the groom's family. In many instances, the new brides are set 'accidentally' on fire.

Om Swaha, a title taken from the first line of the mantra or chant pronounced by the priest for Hindu marriages, opens with the episode I have just described. Rao and feminist director Anuradha Kapur devised the play in 1979 as an agitprop piece in collaboration with women's groups who were mobilizing a public campaign around the issue of dowry deaths, which had reached unprecedented numbers – with very few convictions (Rao, 2021c). According to Rao, this was also the first time 'We made a play' for the larger public, as part of the new women's movement that emerged after the Emergency period in India.[2] Another play was to follow in 1980: *Dafa 180* (*Section 180*). Also agitprop in style, the latter dealt with custodial rape; it was conceived after a horrific incident in which Mathura, a tribal woman, was raped at a police station. *Dafa 180* became part of the women's movement campaign for law reforms against rape.

Massive public campaigns on urgent issues such as dowry deaths, rape, and violence against women from all social classes were led by the women's movement; feminist theatre emerged from within these campaigns. Focussing on *Om Swaha* and *Dafa 180*, I aim to trace Rao's agitprop work in relation to the women's movement – work that she acknowledges as instrumental in shaping her intellectual and artistic life (Rao, 2021c).

2.1 Women's Movement, Public Campaigns, and Agitprop: *Om Swaha*

By the late 1970s, the 'feminist focus' of the women's movement in India was formed by and through the 'growth of "autonomous" women's groups in towns and cities, without party affiliations or formal hierarchical structures, although individual members often had party connections' (Menon, 2012: 19). The dilemma in the new women's movements was how feminist politics could best be conducted: through the urban middle-class orientations of these autonomous groups or by raising women's issues within mass organizations, particularly within the left-wing parties? Consequently, there was fierce debate over the issue of retaining the independent character of autonomous groups, versus the

---

[2] Emergency refers to the period between 1975 and 1977 in India when the government suspended all fundamental rights in the name of internal emergency according to the constitutional provision of Article 352.

affiliations to left-wing parties, where patriarchal structures were deeply rooted. Yet despite these ongoing debates and diverse ways of functioning, a number of feminist campaigns were launched, particularly around the issues of dowry and rape, with different feminists coming together in solidarity to set up women's resources.[3]

Rao and Kapur had been invited by campaigners Subhadra and Urvashi Butalia (mother and daughter) to meet with feminist groups whose members had different skill sets (Kapur and Rao's being theatre) and political interests but found common cause in the struggle against dowry. As Kapur explains, 'there were many overlaps of skills and personalities. Women rallied around the issues ... these were affiliations and collectivities' (Kapur, 2021a). Apart from being a social problem, dowry deaths were also entangled with many personal experiences. In an initial conversation, Subhadra Butalia pointed towards a house in her neighbourhood at Jangpura where a dowry death had recently occurred (Kapur, 2021a). Further, Madhu Kishwar and Ruth Vanita, two feminist scholars and activists involved in the movement, described how the dowry murder of twenty-four-year-old Tavinder Kaur was not, as was generally the case, relegated to a couple of lines in an obscure corner of a daily newspaper but garnered headlines, leading to women's groups organizing processions and demonstrations in front of Kaur's house: 'Tavinder's mother cried but not alone. Many women in Delhi cried out with loud voices' (Kishwar and Vanita, 2008: 42). Placards in the demonstrations read 'Arrest the Killers of Women' or 'We will never give dowry nor let women burn'. 'We need new instruments of consciousness raising if women are to stop seeing themselves as belonging to various families, to various men and begin to see other women as sisters – even though not born of the same biological parents' (Kishwar and Vanita, 2012: 46). It was in this context that *Om Swaha* was created, was staged, and gained immense popularity – it became a byword or mnemonic for the campaign.

The making of *Om Swaha* was a collaborative process. Rao and Kapur listened to the women's extensive deliberations (sometimes for hours). It was challenging to devise a thirty-minute play out of so much debate. Ultimately the play was based on a real-life incident in which two friends died, one after the other, because of dowry. But Rao and Kapur also needed to find a theatrical mode to capture and distil the multifaceted discussions. They devised what they termed formations. The formations, Rao explains, were the pillars or cornerstones which held the play together without any need for a linear, narrative

---

[3] Radha Kumar's *The History of Doing* (2011) and Shamita Sen's 'Towards a Feminist Politics? The Indian Women's Movement in Historical Perspective' (2003) offer overviews of the women's movement in its early years.

structure. Formations were designed as emblematic moments to exemplify key ideas; they involved the play's protagonists and a chorus and were often underscored by a rhythmic text. In between these formations short episodes were performed in a realist mode (Rao, 2021d). Aided by the chorus, formations and episodes blended into one another, mapping transitions of time and space.

After the opening auction of grooms, the chorus moved around in circles, clapping their hands, declaring that marriages had taken place. This was followed by newspaper vendors announcing the sensational news of a girl, Hardeep, being murdered by her in-laws for not fulfilling further dowry demands. A sceptical reporter is out to gather facts but is met with silent neighbours – the chorus sit in a circle looking out like the three wise monkeys who see no evil, hear no evil, and speak no evil. Only Hardeep's friend Kanchan is ready to speak, but her voice is stifled. The next few episodes reveal Hardeep's tragedy: her marriage, how she was tortured and beaten up by her new family, and how on the day of her death she was doused with kerosene and set on fire to make it look like an accident. Now bereft of an unlimited source of income from his bride's family, the husband, with the assistance of his father, is already planning a second marriage. The body of Hardeep, shrouded in black, is carried off by the chorus amidst religious chanting.

Thereafter the play focusses on Kanchan; there is a feeling of déjà vu as she is married off with a dowry despite her protests. The marriage is played as a comedic critique to exemplify how women are commodified, reduced to an economic transaction. But an emblematic moment is altogether darker: the red veil used to cover the head of the bride becomes a whip as the chorus recites the dowry demands:

> Not one lakh, not two lakhs (whiplash)
> Not three lakhs, not five lakhs
> No Fridge, no mixie
> No Iron, no TV (whiplash) . . .
> No earrings, or bangles,
> No footbells, or the nose-ring.
> No father-in-law's shoes, no the brother-in-law's suit
> No Pappu's jersey, no the sister-in-law's saree (whiplash).
> (change in the voice)
> Was she beaten up daily, was she beaten up daily?
> (*Om Swaha*, 1988: 46)

Traumatized by the demands of her in-laws, Kanchan tries to run back home. Rao, playing the role of Kanchan, describes the formation that presented the two families standing in dual rows, while Kanchan ran from one to the other, her own family refusing to take her back and the in-laws continuing with their unfair demands (Rao, 2021d). Literally trapped into marriage and a situation of day-to-day domestic violence, Kanchan figuratively becomes the bull of the bullock cart that carries the burden of her family. A *chunni* (scarf) tied to her chest is held by the rest of her family as she pulls and drags them along. The actress, like Brecht's Mother Courage pulling her wagon, circles the space while almost immobilized by the weight of the actors who start climbing on to her bent back. The chorus changes to the final formation of a *chakki* – a local mechanism where two rounded stone slabs are used for grinding grains; one goes around clockwise and the other anticlockwise (Figure 3). Rao as Kanchan sits in the centre and makes the motion of going around in circles while the chorus goes in the other direction. She appears to be in immense pain and about to collapse, but then she stands up and leaves the *chakki* formation to declare:

> You have seen what happened to me;
> My father kept on doling out dowry –
> My brother on the sly kept on demanding dowry – And the rest of you just watched silently?
> The Sutradhar (interlocutor): But what could I do? It was your personal affair?
> Kanchan: You actually think this is a personal matter? You think the battle can be fought alone?
> The Sutradhar: Do you think it is only an individual's story? Can you fight it alone? Please think.
> The chorus as the collective comes back to show a larger front which will take the struggle forward.
>
> (*Om Swaha*, 1988: 50)

Figure 3 *Om Swaha*: Maya Rao in the final *chakki* scene (Photo by Sheba Chhachhi)

In sum, animated by an energy, a passion for the social cause, *Om Swaha* was stylized, poetic, and theatrical. Rao recollects it as a mise en scène of images, words, sounds, rhythms, and body sculptures (Rao, 2021d). Moreover, crucially all efforts were made to depict Kanchan not as a victim who had no choice other than a dowry marriage, but as a woman who questioned the practice of dowry as a systemic form of violence against women. When she leaves the *chakki* formation and looks directly at the audience to ask, 'how can I remain silent?' the implication is 'how can [we] remain silent?' In short, this was agitprop theatre deployed to urge audiences to feel, think, and reject dowry marriages – to be moved to fight for legal redress rather than accept that women were victims by default.

2.2 Reception, Mobilization, and the Public Campaign

The first performance of *Om Swaha* took place in October 1979 on the Indraprastha (IP) College lawns in Delhi, where two feminist-activist scholars, Kumkum Sangari and Suresh Vaid, were teaching literature. In this context, Kapur points out, a new feminist and gender consciousness was impacting disciplinary shifts (Kapur, 2021a).[4] The IP College performance, as recollected by Rao, was charged with energy; *Om Swaha* went on to be performed more than a hundred times, initially as part of women's marches and demonstrations, and subsequently on college campuses, in parks adjoining places where dowry deaths had occurred, in larger middle-class housing complexes, and at well-known protest sites in Delhi such as the India Gate and the Boat Club.[5] The play would also be taken to other cities, such as Saharanpur and Bombay, as well as being performed at many women's conferences, forums, and meetings.[6] When the piece played in the streets, the performers would create a space amidst the people gathered; the audience would sit in very close proximity to the actors.

---

[4] By 1986, four women's studies centres (in the universities of Kerala, Punjab, and Delhi, and in Benaras Hindu University) were established. By 1997, they numbered twenty-two, and by 2007, there were around sixty-six. Women's studies cells were also established in a few undergraduate women's colleges in Delhi (John, 2008: 13). Kapur and Rao both made the transition to full-time theatre work with a commitment to feminist practices. Both went on to study at the University of Leeds.

[5] The Boat Club and the India Gate, central landmarks of Delhi, face Raisina Hill, the seat of government and the president's palace. The Boat Club was regarded as the national square of resistance until a ban was imposed in the 1990s. In 2021, the Supreme Court reinstated the right to protest at this site.

[6] The plays and the movement between 1980 and 1995 have been extensively documented and photographed by the feminist artist Sheba Chhachhi. I have drawn on this documentation to reconstruct the plays (https://aaa.org.hk/en/collections/search/archive/photo-documentation-of-om-swaha-from-the-sheba-chhachhi-archive).

The divide between the performing space and the audience was porous, and the actors often reached out to their audiences for responses and reactions.

Om Swaha's success or legendary status in the feminist movement, as part of the public campaign amidst protests, demonstrations, and marches, played a particular role: it allowed audiences the space and time to think of the issues and to entertain the idea that social change, an end to dowry deaths, was not only desirable but possible. Audiences were significantly moved to think of these matters when the play was staged where such deaths had occurred. At one show in Model town, the mother of Hardeep Kaur was present in the audience. Rao says she had no prior knowledge but could feel a palpably charged atmosphere that day, and, after the performance, the mother put her head on her lap and thumped her body as if to bring her dead daughter back to life, crying all the while (Rao, 2021d). There were also instances of hostility towards the actors and activists, but, on occasion, as Kapur explains, initial hostilities could be overcome through engagement with the play (Kapur, 2021a).

2.3 Critique of the Women's Movement and Continuing Violence

Om Swaha's reception clearly evidences the play as a success story of the campaign. But on what terms can either the play or the campaign be argued as impactful when the issue of dowry violence and deaths persisted? This kind of question, criticism even, is frequently levelled at the women's movement in tandem with accusations of an upper-middle-class and urban bias. Feminists have tried to counter the latter by proving how the movement encompassed a large number of organizations in many regions of India, including those affiliated with left-wing organizations. The former cannot be answered or countered by the citation of empirical data. The answer lies elsewhere: in the feminist consciousness raising achieved through the play and the campaign that heightened awareness not only of the dowry issue, but crucially also of the patriarchal culture that underpins it.

In defence of *Om Swaha's* impact, Uma Chakravarti in her essay titled 'Cultures of Resistance: The Women's Movement in Performance' cites how the play's conception and staging acknowledged the cultural production of violence. Further, it is also important to note how *Om Swaha* resonated with agitprop plays from other organizations such as Jana Natya Manch's *Aurat* (*Woman*) (1979), Sachetana's plays in Bengal with *Meye Dile Sajiye* (*Giving the Women Away in Marriage*) (1983), *Mulqi Zhali Hai* (*A Girl Is Born*) (1983), and *Roshni* by Manushi (1980).[7] Together these could be regarded as a diverse field

---

[7] *Nukkad*, volumes 1 and 2, are issues devoted to women-oriented street theatre; they include play texts, interviews, and articles.

of feminist activism in different parts of the country. Raka Ray explains that this is important if we are to see the feminist movement not only as a social movement limited to mobilization or the opening up of political opportunities, but also as what she argues is a relational field fostering a political and protest culture, one that is valuable to feminist consciousness raising (Ray, 2000: 7).

Kumkum Sangari, a feminist scholar and one of the important leaders of the anti-dowry movement, accuses those who criticize feminist engagement with gendered violence as uncritically assuming a culturalist position:

> Such culturalism works as a code for tradition and religion, conflates religion and patriarchies with 'culture' and turns acts of violence into religion driven Third World pathologies or customary/sacred traditions. This complicates feminist attempts to critique violent practices, especially since culturalist accounts also tend to spectacularize and decontextualize violent acts. (Sangari, 2012: 325)

Thus Sangari articulates the issue of gendered violence as a fundamental and systematic feature of patriarchies, often entangled with the social, cultural, and political economy and regarded as synonymous with belief systems. The feminist concern with dowry practice, she further elucidates, is closely related to material considerations, the uneven distribution of labour and resources, exploitative production relations, control of reproductive bodies, articulation of caste and class, and the logics of capitalism (Sangari, 2012: 326–7). The agitprop mode of *Om Swaha* was an attempt to include all these elements; as Rao claims, it created the opportunity to think, understand, and discuss dowry in the context of larger issues to do with the status of women in the family and society (Rao, 2021d).

Sangari's argument indicates that what was essential to the women's movement was the understanding and need to communicate that patriarchy is not merely a matter of men ruling women, but that it is implicated in the deeper social fabric. This is particularly the case in the practice of dowry within the familial unit; the violence related to it is often unleashed with women's consent or with women as active agents, as reflected in *Om Swaha*'s depiction of the mother-in-law who is complicit in accepting dowry. (The mother who sends Kanchan back to her in-laws is also responsible for upholding tradition.) Sangari argues that the active complicity of women can be attributed to various factors such as the 'anticipation of violence, or the guarantee of violence in the last instance to ensure obedience, inculcate submission and punish transgression' (Sangari, 2012: 326). To critique this violence is essential because:

> [V]iolence forces us to think that the point of breakdown of love, protection and familial bonds in violent acts is the point at which patriarchal power is

reassembled and family, community and the state are reinscribed as patriarchal institutions. Therefore violence is not only one of the points of
reproduction, but, ironically also the point at which the faultlines of
a patriarchal system are policed. (Sangari, 2012: 328)

In sum, for Sangari and women engaged in the movement, violence is a political
act which operates as a nexus between the family, community, state, and cultural
institutions and needs to be challenged.

By organizing public campaigns on women's issues, the women's movement
tried to expose the violence occurring in the domestic space, often thus providing
immunity to the perpetrators. Such campaigns insisted that the private (domestic)
and public structures of violence are connected to each other; the political patriarchal powers are implicated in forms of inequality and are made visible through
dowry demands, marital rape, or domestic oppression. In this regard, the agitprop
style of *Om Swaha* sought to demonstrate the links between traditional or specific
violence and non-cultural, everyday oppression. Agitprop was also important to
building feminist solidarities: dramatizing and demonstrating issues in ways that
could reach across differences in class or in urban or rural settings. What *Om
Swaha* did *not* do was to tell audiences what they should do; rather the performance
served to create discussion forums. Feminist groups often came forward as the play
ended, with pamphlets providing helpline numbers and pointing out mechanisms
of redress to counter such violence. Maya Rao recollects how, while playing
Kanchan, she found it difficult to deal with the trauma of the impending dowry
death with which the play ended, how she felt that she could not provide answers
for women who experience such violence on a daily basis. For her, it was a question
of getting under the skin of those women (Rao, 2021d). Theatrically, that was how
Om Swaha also functioned – inviting audiences to feel-see not only the issue of
dowry, but also the structures of patriarchal violence impacting women's daily
lives.

2.4 Campaign against Sexual Violence and *Dafa 180*

From the issue of dowry, the women's movement turned to another urgent
matter – that of custodial rape and related issues of sexual violence. The
prevalence of sexual violence against women was a major concern for Indian
feminists; it came to the fore when Mathura, a tribal woman, was brutally raped
in police custody on 26 March 1972. A subsequent Supreme Court judgment
acquitted the police-rapists. The women's movement launched a massive public
campaign against the flawed judgment, demanding the modification of anti-
quated laws which acquitted the accused (Sections 375 and 376 of the Indian
Penal code, unchanged since 1860 (Menon, 2011: 109)). Consequently, the

government was compelled to set up a law commission to recommend modifications. Rao and Kapur devised *Dafa 180* (*Section 180*) to coincide with a massive demonstration to be held in front of the Law Commission in 1980.

Kumkum Sangari, Suresh Vaid, and other women's groups (about eight of them) again provided Rao and Kapur, now working with the Theatre Union, the data and information required to create a play.[8] The aim was to capture the experience of violence but also to create a discursive space, focussing on rights or on the existing means to seek protection from such violence, and the lacunae in the legal system. Working with the Theatre Union, Rao and Kapur initiated a collaborative workshop process. *Dafa 180* evolved to depict three scenarios where rape was a common phenomenon: in urban settings and institutions, in rural locations particularly amongst the Nepani *bidi* (cigarette) workers where the local landlords unleashed sexual violence on a frequent basis, and individual cases. The data provided by the women's groups was supplemented by information from the actors. Two doctors who were members of the Theatre Union and worked at Delhi's biggest public hospital (Safdarjung) informed the group about their experiences with patients they had examined and treated after sexual violence, some of them infants or young children. The play therefore had more leeway to combine experience and affect with the discursive and was a key initiative in a movement increasingly geared towards seeking legal redress and justice (Rao, 2021d).

That said, the first performance of *Dafa 180* in front of the Law Commission exemplified the tension between the aspiration to transform entrenched patriarchal structures and the feminist movement's preoccupation with judicial processes. In *Recovering Subversion: Feminist Politics beyond the Law*, Nivedita Menon highlights how the movement's preoccupation with the legal process was at the expense of other related issues that delved deeper into structural violence and patriarchy. In terms of sexual violence against women, she also asks an important question about how violence is inscribed on women's bodies: 'What are the codes that enable such immediate recognition of "sexuality" and "sexual" violence? Are they indeed so universally recognized by all cultures, by all women? And in this recognition, . . . does it paradoxically, *limit* the possibilities of feminist transformation?' (Menon, 2011: 106). Hence Menon interrogates what causes sexually violent acts to be accepted as a precondition that requires the intervention of the judicial process, or what will convince a law commission set up by the state in the face of protests.

---

[8] In 1979, Kapur and Rao along with Manohar Kushlani and Ragini Sen formed the Theatre Union as a company dedicated to theatre activism. According to Kapur, this created a way for them to devote more time to devising and performing plays (Kapur, 2021a). The group maintained links to feminist organizations.

The Law Commission, for example, did recommend the main demand of the feminists – that in rape cases, the onus of proving consent should shift from the woman who had been violated to the accused. But the Criminal Law Amendment Act, passed in 1983, accepted this demand only partially: it would be applicable only in the case of custodial rape. Also, the mandatory minimum punishment was made more rigorous. However, as Menon points out elsewhere, more stringent laws seen as restraints also make convictions more difficult (Menon, 2012: 23). Menon summarizes her concerns as twofold: firstly, the sexism of the legal system, where the culpability of the accused and the violation of the victim had to be established, resulting in the legal procedure often degenerating into misogyny; secondly, the legal system's failure to acknowledge how the body and sex are not natural but projected through discourses. Further, she argues that such difficulties were compounded by the way in which feminist campaigns narrowed in scope as they focussed more and more on legal processes and law reforms and sought to negotiate with the state and the judiciary, thereby 'suturing the open endedness' of the movement (Menon, 2011: 107).[9]

Dafa 180 recognized these problems and contradictions and, I would argue, took on board how to codify the rape act and the embodiment of sexual violation in ways that eschewed playing the victim in a conventional recognizable style. To explain how *Dafa 180* refrained from victim-playing, Rao and Kapur expound on the climactic scenes in which sexual violence is depicted. They describe how this had to be dramatic to hold the attention of the audience yet also had to avoid showing the woman as nothing more than a victim. Instead, it was important to depict her as someone who could resist and assert her position against such violations. And yet they also had to avoid creating an unrealistic, improbable scenario in which the protagonist stood up for her rights and saved herself (Kapur, 2021a; Rao, 2021d). Ultimately, it was a question of finding a more oblique way of showing the victim as a survivor. To exemplify this, at the end of the scenario depicting the rape of *bidi* workers, Rao devised a formation with ropes. Men and women stood in a jagged line, holding a thick rope, with Rao as the female worker facing sexual violence and frantically trying to escape. She became increasingly entangled in its twirls and swirls (Figure 4).

In the final rape act, there was another formation of the circle, but enacted only by men, each representing an institution of power and authority such as the police, state, landowners, or corporations, each loudly proclaiming their identity. The woman/Rao was again trapped in the centre. The men threw feet bells

---

[9] Over the past four decades, rape laws and trials have emerged as a significant site of feminist engagement. Pratiksha Baxi's *Public Secrets of Law: Rape Trials in India* (2014) offers a detailed account of court ethnographies of such trials.

Figure 4 *Dafa 180*: The formation with ropes (Photo by Sheba Chhachhi)

(*ghungroos*), a mass of small, round bells, at each other and adopted different attitudes and poses – teasing, seductive, often building in momentum and laced with violence. In the centre, the woman/Rao tried to avoid being hit by the bells, even trying to catch them, running desperately within the confines of the circle. In both scenarios, the woman was in motion; her movements gained momentum. Thus, in their depiction and strategic deployment of the woman's body in motion, rather than at a standstill, these enactments can be seen as an alternative to conventional representations of the passive, victimized body: the trauma of sexual violence, as rendered by Rao, also embodied resistant gestures.

In examining the role of public campaigns on dowry deaths and sexual violence and agitprop theatre that was integral to the women's movement, I have looked to understand if theatre with its dramaturgy, performative idioms, and processes had the potential that Menon emphasizes to validate women's experiences as more diverse, 'open-ended', rather than 'uniform'. If 'uniform' in one way due to their agitprop address of a particular issue – dowry in the case of *Om Swaha*, rape in *Dafa 180* – these performances by Rao and Kapur also reflect an 'open endedness' as they variously tug at the multiple threads that weave patriarchy through the social fabric, initiate consciousness raising, and create opportunities for conversations between artists, activists, and audiences who identified with the issues and the feminist movement at large. That work was of its time, but as the next section on the Nirbhaya rape case (2012) and Rao's *Walk* will show, the need for feminist activism and dialogue in India has not diminished.

3 *Walk* and Its Multiple Trajectories

On 29 December 2012, Jyothi Singh, known as Nirbhaya (the Fearless), passed away as a result of a bodily assault perpetrated on her during a brutal rape. The public outcry that followed the attack on 16 December 2012, while Singh struggled for her life in the hospital but with her spirit unbroken, called for action. Angry women, young and old, feminists, activists, university students, and many others gathered every day to protest and brought the city to a halt. This demonstration is often cited as the Indian counterpart to the anti-authoritarianism, anti-capitalist protests spreading all over the world after 2011, such as Occupy Wall Street in New York, the Arab Spring demonstrations, Gunduz the dancer-choreographer standing in stoic silence in Taksim Square in Istanbul, protesters at Tahrir Square in Cairo, the emergence of Black Lives Matter, and student protests. However, the demonstration in India was different in the sense that it centred on sexual violence against women.

As noted in Section 2, sexual violence has been a key issue for Indian feminism. In the forty-year gap separating the rape of Mathura in 1972 and the fatal rape of Singh in 2012, sexual violence had not ceased; rather it had increased. On the other hand, from the 1980s onwards, as neoliberal reforms were implemented in India, the autonomous organizations of earlier times that spearheaded the movements against dowry and rape lost touch with grass-root campaigns. These groups had transformed themselves into non-governmental organizations (NGOs) funded by state, corporate, and foreign sources (Menon, 2011: 220). They dealt with specific issues such as abortion, family planning, social rehabilitation, sex trafficking, and economic self-reliance. Thus, feminism was reduced to dealing with social issues specific to women, rather than opposing the all-pervading patriarchal structures in a larger political field, as earlier feminist projects had aspired to do. This begins to explain why Rao and Kapur moved away from being the public face of feminist campaigns to pursue careers in the theatre (Section 5).

Elsewhere, Menon lamented, 'We no longer seem to think it necessary to challenge our notions of "self" and "Identity". It is as if we know what "feminism" is, and only need to apply it unproblematically to specific instances' (Menon, 2011: 220). But when sexual violence came to the fore after the attack on Singh in 2012, as Anupama Roy explains, it 'assumed criticality by becoming a part of incremental accumulation of memories of gendered violence' (Roy, 2014: 238).

When news of the attack broke, protestors gathered at a number of sites in the city of Delhi, including landmark buildings, monuments, and the bus stop where Nirbhaya boarded the bus on which the attack took place. There was no orchestrated move on the part of feminists to protest. Rather, women like Rao felt compelled to join the crowds, march, and chant slogans for justice – they found solace in just being with large groups of so many women walking the streets:

> To see these young boys and girls marching up and down with India Gate at one end and Rashtrapati Bhavan at the other end, many of them for the first time, . . . making up their single slogan, which just went on and on, 'We want justice, We want justice' as if they were in a trance and the women's organizations, student organizations and older women following behind them, it really transformed me and the city of Delhi in some ways. (Rao quoted in Ghosh, 2014: 156)[10]

The coming together of women (and men) from diverse sections of society, touching each other as 'norms of appropriate proximity dissolved, conventional hierarches collapsed' (Dean, 2018: 120), was a collective experience. This was in stark contrast to neoliberalism's vaunting of individualism.

The attack and the protests galvanized Rao into creating her landmark performance, *Walk* – a ten-minute poetically and rhythmically voiced demand to end sexual violence against women. Rao performed *Walk* to a musical accompaniment that patterned and amplified her resistant gestures and speech (the full description follows in Section 3.1). *Walk* was first staged at midnight on 31 December 2012 at a park in Munirka, Delhi. Those who gathered for the performance included students and faculty from Jawaharlal Nehru University (JNU), activists, feminists, and a large crowd of people from the city, all of whom had turned out despite the biting cold and foggy winter night. A few days later, Rao performed *Walk* to a massive audience at Jantar Mantar as the protests in the city intensified.[11] Amidst the shock of the attack and the collective mourning, *Walk* struck a feminist note of struggle and assertiveness – an echo of *Dafa 180*.

Centred on the issue of sexual violence, *Walk* highlights the unresolved issues of the feminist movement, particularly in the age of globalization and neo-liberalism. The neoliberal policies and economic reforms implemented since the 1980s, which invited foreign investment and involved massive reforms of state and governance, had weakened the social democratic state. The govern-ment had divested itself of developmental programmes, social responsibilities, and welfare support. This was disastrous for a country like India given its large, economically vulnerable population. And in the case of women, a weakened

---

[10] Ghosh is quoting from Rao's speech at the Jaipur literary festival where she performed *Walk* on 28 January 2013.

[11] Jantar Mantar is a historical site in central Delhi built between 1724 and 1730 as an astronomical observatory. Adjoining the site is a space demarcated for protests in recent years.

feminist movement, as previously described, was not in a position to challenge the social and economic inequalities that deepened under neoliberalism.

Moreover, and more specifically, the 2012 protests were not organized by feminist groups as part of a public campaign, and neither was *Walk* (unlike *Dafa 180*) offered as part of a campaign programme. To grasp the importance of these differences to earlier feminist protests and campaigning, we might think of how Menon describes the possibilities of political (feminist) practice as a scenario in which neoliberal policies and a weakened state and social welfare priorities create a crisis as patriarchy, sexism, communalism, and casteism reach unprecedented heights. She argues, that 'Our understanding should become the common sense – that should be our political goal. In short, the project of a radical democratic practice is nothing less than the hegemonizing of common sense' (Menon, 2011: 239). Following Menon, 'the hegemonizing of common sense' in respect of women's issues is the means by which feminism might regain traction as a 'radical democratic practice', serving as an impulse or a catalyst to raise feminist issues in the public domain and the larger social and political fields. If the performances of *Walk* are significant, it is because they capture the common sense of women who want to be free of sexual violence, who want to 'walk' freely on the streets. In other words, *Walk*'s feminist orientation stems from the populist demands and sentiments voiced or felt by women gathered at the performance sites. And by translating the democratic impulses of the protests into a performance, *Walk* functions as a conduit for common sense, popular sentiments, to align with feminist activism. With its forceful steps, assertive gestures, and upbeat text (see Section 3.1), *Walk* embodied the protest experience, rather than the trauma of sexual violence.

Since the initial performance of *Walk*, Rao has created various versions in which she brings out different meanings and intonations. In brief, *Walk* has gone through shifts and transitions as Rao has looked to respond to a broad range of issues, performing the piece at colleges and universities, literature festivals and book fairs, and in her repertoire of solo theatre-based performances (see Section 5). All versions of *Walk* between 2012 and 2016 embodied modes of resistance to an increasingly conservative India at a time when feminist issues were re-emerging in the public sphere. It also mapped with the emergence of new protest sites of gatherings and congregations – those that Judith Butler posits as new and innovative trends of assemblage (Butler, 2015). In the context of neoliberalism, under which social movements, civil institutions, and left-wing political parties are weakened, protest activism could be regarded as a radical strategy and an enduring form of democratic citizenship. Anupama Roy regards the way in which protests transform public spaces as a significant example of how 'the complexity of powerlessness . . . may be mapped in terms of the potentials it has for making radical democratic citizenship possible' (Roy, 2016: 185). Following Roy, what we were therefore witnessing were new modes of radical democratic articulations in contemporary neoliberal times. To put this another way, this was a manifestation of what Butler describes as 'embodied and plural performativity' (Butler, 2015: 8), where 'acting in concert can be an embodied form of calling into question the inchoate and powerful dimensions of reigning notions of the political' (Butler, 2015: 9).[12]

3.1 *Walk*, a Performance Strategy

The first version of *Walk,* performed during the protests, was a call to fight and eliminate sexual violence from the lives of women. Here is Rao's now famous appeal to walk:

> Gimme gimme gimme gimme gimme gimme gimme . . .
> Give me a street, safe enough to walk in,
> Give me, give me a cop, a policeman
> I can put my trust in
> Give me a law, that one law
> that sets me free.[13]

As is evident from Rao's rhythmically composed lines of protest, *Walk* was designed to provoke action: to call for defiance, to fight back, and to demand legal redress. With a music track playing in the background against her poetic recitation, Rao set the rhythm of a walk; it was bold and strong. The audience matched her steps. The collective experience of walking was not only mesmerizing, but an antidote to the grief and mourning for Singh. Rao recalls:

> In uttering 'walk' I try to simultaneously sense the bodily action of the leg slowly going up, as if I am doing it for the first time in my life, to sense what it means to cover ground, both in terms of physical space and ask myself if I am ready to open spaces in my mind, to find in that instant a connection with the audience – that I am doing an action that we take for granted because ALL of us do at some point of the day . . . everyday . . . to celebrate the fact that my (our) simple capacity to put one leg after the other means I can reach all corners of the world, that Jyoti will never enjoy again and so I must try and do it for her, that one step leads to the next and the next. In fact, for me the thought 'I want the freedom to walk unhindered' is only one part of it. (quoted in Ghosh, 2014: 184)

---

[12] The Nirbhaya protests and performance manifestations have received extensive scholarly attention from performance, feminist, and political studies scholars such as Arora (2019a, 2019b, 2020), Durham (2014), Dutt (2015, 2017), Leider (2015), Patil and Purkayastha (2018), and Roy (2014, 2016).
[13] Transcribed from a personal recording, 31 December 2012.

Setting aside shame and stigma, *Walk* renews the call for structural changes, a dismantling of patriarchal power in both private and public domains:

> It's a new year
> We all have to
> Walk walk, walk walk walk … (Walk is repeated many times, with the strides.)
> I'll walk all night,
> …
> I sit in a bus,
> I'll cross the road,
> I'll lie in the park,
> I'm not afraid of the dark.

As these lines reflect, *Walk* advocates a notion of freedom for women that encompasses access to public spaces, the right to public life that they are denied.

Rao continues by highlighting a key concern with respect to sexual violence: consent. If men want to fight gender violence, then they must, her lines repeatedly insist, abide by the notion of consent:

> And I'll hear the dark, whisper whisper whisper whisper,
> Can you hear that …
> I'll tell you what it says..
> When you want to talk, you must ask her
> When you want to sit with her,
> You must ask her,
> If you want to have sex with her, you have to first ask her …
> And tomorrow, if you are getting married to her
> Please ask her,
> Pucho na yaar
> Just ask once,
> Just ask.

In *Walk*, Rao is not only a witness to the trauma, but is one of the many who walk and talk with those who are all around; it is the call to walk and talk together that forges feminist solidarities. In solidarity with her audience, Rao reaches out to the people around her, bending down, inviting them on stage, or gesturing to them with open arms. What is distinctive about her bodily/textual gestures is their capacity to mark and protest present and past injustices, but also to capture a sense of the reparative. In *Theory for Theatre Studies: Memory*, Milija Gluhovic posits performance as a medium to recover lost or blocked memories – performance as a dynamic exchange between life and the stage that fuels theatre's capacity to be a reparative ground for empathetic encounters through small acts of repair and 'an attempt to shift the inexorable negativity of death drive, and its will to destruction, in a more productive and moral direction'

(Gluhovic, 2020: 48). Following Gluhovic, Rao's *Walk* can be understood as recovering memories of violence, but with a view to reparative and affirmative action.

After Rao's first *Walk* at the protest sites, she began to perform the piece extensively in colleges and universities, in theatres alongside her solo shows like *Non Stop Feel Good Show*, or at numerous commemorations particularly on the anniversary of 16 December 2012 (Figure 5). Performing on the first anniversary, Rao reached out gently to young women who had once marched on the streets, reminding them that the struggle must continue until the patriarchal foundations of society change. She still moves among her audiences, often holding out her hands, gently touching women in a caring way, and adds lines such as 'Give me a mother, who can stand up against a mama [maternal uncle], or a chacha [paternal uncle] – can stand by the side of her daughter', referring to the underlying day-to-day violence women face within households where patriarchy is institutionalized and harassment often goes unnoticed or suppressed. In short, always geared towards resilience and resistance, Rao's *Walk* continues to fulfil the function of feminist performance activism – raising feminist consciousness.

Strident and resistant, Rao's performances of *Walk* refused to memorialize Nirbhaya as a victim. This was in stark contrast to the way in which, as the legal process against her attackers unfolded, the media constructed women's sexuality in terms of victimhood, placing an emphasis on chastity, morality, and gender norms according to Indian traditions. While demanding justice, the media coverage increasingly focussed on the violated body, referring to

Figure 5 On the first anniversary of *Walk*, Maya Rao at the JNU night vigil
(Photo by Priyam Ghosh)

Nirbhaya as India's daughter and re-enacting the crime over and over again, showing the location and voicing how she was found naked here too with a focus on the violated body and a commentary that bordered on misogyny in order to evoke outrage.

This mode of 'policing' women's sexuality is also mirrored in rape trials where, as Menon explains, legal language codifies and regulates women's bodies in terms of victimhood (Menon, 2011: 107); it re-enacts and recements patriarchal and misogynist values (Menon 2012: 284). She elaborates on how the issue of sexual violence, in the judicial process as well as in the mainstream media, becomes one of 'proving the magnitude of rape or sexual violence' (Menon 2012: 290). And between the media hype and the law, securing a conviction becomes increasingly dependent on the perceived guilt or innocence of the victim. All of this is antithetical to the emancipatory, feminist impulse that underscored Rao's performance: the right to 'walk' in safety demands women's freedom from patriarchal control, regulation, and violation.

3.2 The LGBTQ Movement and a New Version of *Walk*: *377 Ways to Love*

Among the different iterations of *Walk*, I want to single out Rao's adaptation of the piece for the Day of Rage at Jantar Mantar on 15 December 2013, immediately following the Supreme Court's rejection of the Delhi High Court's recommendation to strike off Article 377 as unconstitutional.[14] Article 377, an obsolete colonial law, while acknowledging that homosexuality per se is not an offence, states that sodomy (whether heterosexual or homosexual) can be classified as a crime (John, 2008: 560). Article 377 has been invoked to harass and threaten gay men, lesbians, and bisexual women.

The Day of Rage was organized nationwide and globally. Rao was invited to perform *Walk* at the demonstration in Delhi, arranged, like all the Day of Rage events, to demonstrate opposition to the regressive judgment and to raise public awareness.[15] Butler insightfully points out that campaigns on the streets are not only about agitating against a law. They also yield more far-reaching effects such as raising consciousness around inclusion through building solidarities.

---

[14] www.youtube.com/watch?v=ySjoUTUAwmU&t=9s.

[15] In 2009, the Delhi High Court, on a petition filed by the Naz Foundation, had ruled that Section 377 of the Indian Penal Code (IPC) was unconstitutional, but public morality petitions filed by religious and other groups resulted in the case being taken to the Supreme Court, where Justice Sanghvi set aside the 2009 decision. Subsequently, in *Navtej Johar and others* v. *Union of India* in 2018, once again an appeal was made to the Supreme Court when Section 377 was finally unanimously declared unconstitutional 'in so far as it criminalises consensual sexual conduct between adults of the same sex'. For more details and earlier petitions, see Ankush Gupta, 'Pink Nights' (Unpublished M.Phil. dissertation), 2012.

Making a distinction between the legal process and public campaigns, she emphasizes that the legal process requires conditions of appearance and only an elite few can appear before the law or in courts (Butler 2015: 40–1), as per the appearance of the Naz Foundation or subsequently Navtej Johar in 2018.[16] In contrast, those who were present at the public gatherings across the country were diverse and heterogeneous groups.

For her Day of Rage performance, Rao appeared on stage with her back to the audience. She was clad in a black saree with a red border; her white hair was loose and flowing. She turned around as the music track started, taking one step at a time, in a stylized manner, in slow motion, keeping each foot suspended in the air far longer than necessary:

> I step that way, this way, this way, that way,
> One step at a time

The music played on. Rao continued to step and pause her text until, in a loud voice, with her arms apart, she voiced the lines:

> I don't know how to step back anymore
> Because I'm not straight anymore.

Some lines from the original walk then came back with new meanings, a focus on different forms of love and relationships:

> You didn't teach me to how to walk
> How will you ever teach me how to love?

Playing with different syntaxes, rhythms, and expressions, Rao moved easily from empathy, through disappointment and hope, to agitation. In a challenging tone, she uttered:

> Gimme gimme gimme gimme
> This year, 2014, give me 377 days of the year
> 'Cause I have no fear
> So if it takes 377 days
> Then it takes more than 377 ways to … love
> To have sex … give me more

She repeated the final question again, shifting from a defiant tone, to ask in a gentle way, 'How will you ever teach me how to love?'

---

[16] Since 2000, the LGBTQ communities through NGOs and civil society institutions have increasingly led public campaigns for their rights. Ankush Gupta regards the NGOs which steered the campaign as an outcome of Western donor practices in the Global South who funded these campaigns and sometimes made it a precondition (Gupta, 2012: 6–8).

She urged 377 divers ways to be allowed to love. Her message was clear. 'Wherever it takes us – on the streets, at home, in bed', it is important to bring Article 377 to an end. The performance lasted only ten minutes, but it was highly impactful. The politically charged atmosphere among those gathered for the performance/demonstration registered a palpable determination to continue the fight.

Rao's choice of a saree for this performance was an interesting one: a sign of traditional femininity presented to a gay audience for whom she is an icon on account of her customary androgynous appearance. On reflection, I feel this choice was possibly made to press home her point about solidarity across different constituencies. That said, performing *Walk*, Rao constantly disrupts gender norms. She reverts to some stylized idioms from her Kathakali dance repertoire to make feminine gestures with her hands and fingers, referred to as *mudras*, while maintaining masculine postures such as legs wide apart, bold steps, and movements.[17] She thus achieves an interplay of stereotypical codes of masculinity and femininity. At the same time, because she takes idioms from Kathakali, this also highlights the artificiality of its coded forms. The gestures and postures she deploys seem so exaggerated and excessive that they unravel how normative bodies are constructed, installed, and enacted. All told, to watch the presentation is to see the artifice of gender 'norms', especially through the recourse to the classical, codified body of Kathakali.

At the close of the performance, Rao suddenly bent her arms wide apart, a gesture designed to gather all those assembled into one, inclusive embrace. Exiting on this inclusive gesture, she said, 'I can count with you, I can count beyond 377, I will turn the corner.' We can take two meanings from this: the desire for the LGBT community to overcome its own divides and exclusionary strategies such as their antagonistic relations with other sexual minorities, and solidarity between the LGBTQ community and Rao, who identifies herself as a feminist.

As an icon of the LGBTQ community and a performer identified with feminism and the women's movement, Rao is aptly positioned to argue the need for synergies between the two. It is important to note that the LGBTQ and feminist movements in India have a long history of separation, even distrust. This partly stems from a hesitancy on the part of the feminist movement to address women's sexuality. Only during the sixth women's conference at Ranchi in 1997 was a resolution passed: 'We seek the right to make choices about our lives, our bodies, our sexuality

---

[17] Kathakali is one of the four dance forms designated as classical by the Sangeet Natak Akademi in the 1960s. It is a theatrical stylized form, depicting narratives from the epics, and has been an area of interest for performance studies scholars who regard it as an authentic Indian theatrical practice (e.g. Farley Richmond (1993), Richard Schechner (2004), and Philip B. Zarrili (2000, 1984)).

and our relationships ... Some of us have our primary emotional/sexual/physical/ intimate relationships with men, others with women, and some with both. ... We feel that we must evolve supportive structures that can make all of these choices a meaningful reality' (quoted in Menon, 2012: 25). But 'supportive structures' for non-heterosexual relations have been difficult to establish, while, as Menon explains, little was done to address the institutionalization of heterosexuality which dominates patriarchal social structures and works to the detriment of women's sexuality and relationships.

In *Walk*, the need for overcoming divides was spatially reflected in how different communities gathered for the performance: Rao the feminist-LGBTQ icon on an elevated stage, male gay members of the community and the organizers around the stage in a close circle, lesbians in an outer space, and the transgendered community and other sexual minorities left at the margins, even barricaded off from the enclosure. Ankush Gupta has argued that the globalized networks fostering a totalizing LGBTQ identity, particularly among privileged, elite members of a community, are instrumental in marginal-izing sexual minority groups who identify themselves by sexual practices which would not be considered as LGBTQ (Gupta, 2012: 10).

In theorizing the new democratic practices of the streets and speaking on gender performativity, Butler advocates critical coalitional politics that happen on the ground: an interdependency based on alliances between precarious groups and gender minorities that constitute a 'set of enabling and dynamic relations that include support, dispute, breakage, joy and solidarity' (Butler, 2015: 27). Ultimately, it is in this sense that the import of Rao's Day of Rage performance can be best assessed: a 'walk' mobilized in the fight against Article 377 that called for a coalitional politics on the ground.

Of course, such divides cannot be overcome on the strength of one perform-ance. Parenthetically, however, I should note grounds for optimism. For instance, in December 2013, while the LGBTQ community was holding public meetings on Article 377, there were widescale commemorations of the first anniversary of the Nirbhaya incident with participation from feminist and LGBTQ groups – a sign, perhaps, of a coming together in these spaces of new radical practices.

3.3 Back in JNU: *Walk out Sedition*

Three years after her first performance of *Walk* at JNU, Rao walked stealthily down a set of steps where students were sitting, evoking memories of her first walk in a nearby site (see Figure 6):[18]

---

[18] www.youtube.com/watch?v=vxMsVeyzWmU.

Figure 6 *Walk out Sedition*: Maya Rao back at JNU (Photo by Sameem Asgor Ali)

In this JNU, three years ago, on 31 December, we walked, she walked, they walked.

. . .

We walked, we talked, we danced we moved, we fought, we walked.

I am describing the *Walk* performed on 15 February 2016 at what was coming to be known as Freedom Square at JNU.[19] Here was a new crisis: three students, including the Student Union president, were arrested on charges of sedition.[20] The right-wing government under the Bhartiya Janata Party (BJP) and Prime Minister Narendra Modi, who had come to power in 2014, along with the JNU administration, right-wing student organizations, and some media houses were trying to curb the liberal thinking and progressive student politics for which JNU is known. A programme organized by the Democratic Students Union (DSU) titled 'A country without a post office' (referring to Kashmir) had sparked hostilities among those opposed to JNU's liberal ethos. This led to what Ayesha Kidwai described as the university's progressive factions being 'under siege by the police and the self-proclaimed "nationalists" who indulged in and incited violence against the JNU community and the people standing in solidarity' (quoted in Parameswaran, 2016: 1).[21] What followed was a hate campaign against students and the university, labelling it as anti-national.

---

[19] Freedom Square is the popular reference to the space facing the administrative building and the vice chancellor's office. It has a flight of steps where students sat on a daily basis, demanding the release of arrested students and freedom of speech.
[20] The sedition law, Section 124 A of the IPC, is an 1860 colonial law used by governments to suppress dissent.
[21] http://kafila.org/2016/02/13/jnu-under-seige-ayesha-kidwai.

The city and the country were polarized between support for JNU and the hate campaign fuelled by the media, state, and diverse public opinion. Inside the campus the students sat in protest, went on strike, and gathered daily at the steps of the administrative building. Open classes were held and performances took place. The most significant aspect of the students' protest was its 'militancy, self-discipline and conscious efforts to care for the collective and the creative' (Parameswaran, 2016: 3).

Rao, who had come to JNU for a student seminar, at a moment's notice agreed to perform *Walk*, improvising and making it relevant to the crisis. Making her way down the stairs, she said the lines she has recited many times, but she added new lines:

> We will walk
> I'll go down these stairs,
> I will return,
> I will sit, I will discuss
> We'll think together all night
> What's to be done next . . .
> If they didn't teach me how to walk
> How can they teach me where this walk should take me?
> Don't walk with them, we'll walk together.
> Don't talk to them, we'll talk together.

By repeating 'we' several times, she was addressing the students around her. These were students who were in the midst of an unprecedented political crisis, students who would subsequently speak, fight, and 'walk' together to preserve the democratic values of the university and the country. It was not a moment to create friends and enemies but to mobilize solidarities and encourage collectivity. Walking down the stairs, Rao reached out as if to foster friendship, comradeship, and relations. However, doing so, she also stressed the importance of consent – the need to maintain boundaries despite proximity. For Rao, gender sensitivity demands collaboration, egalitarianism, and coalition-making.

In the view of Ameet Parameswaran, this performance particularly elicited questions about how what he calls 'an intimate-public community' might be formed through the performance, how bonds might be cemented among a diverse student group. He asks:

> What is it to perform amidst the protesting students, while selectively edited and doctored images are beamed to the whole nation within the frame of a violent discourse of nationalism? What is it to perform in solidarity, to speak aloud alongside the dissenting students in such precarious conditions? Can performance offer a momentary space of intimate-public community, and can it break through the boundaries of the discursive frame? (Parameswaran, 2016: 2)

According to Parameswaran, the performance was impactful not because it enabled the students' viewpoint to resonate in the larger public domain, but because it facilitated the making of solidarities among the students – it enabled them to emerge as a collective entity and a cohesive group. While the crisis in hand brought the outraged students out to protest on a daily basis, sustaining the protests (they continued for more than a month) depended on them being able to talk through issues, identify common concerns, direct their anger, and resolve to remain together to protest, much as they had done in the 'intimate-public community' forged through Rao's performance. Today, the 2016 events at JNU can be viewed as among the first of many protests against the conservative state led by the BJP – a protest that again benefitted from the politicizing energies generated by Rao's feminist-activist performance.

It is hard to assess the overall impact of Rao's *Walk* in its three-year journey from the Nirbhaya protest through the LGBTQ campaign to the crisis at JNU. However, following Butler, I have sought to argue that these performative moments staged in public assemblies are a 'precondition of politics' (Butler, 2015: 160). In such assemblies, Butler detects the possibility of a shift in the conceptual framework to understand the freedom of assemblies and indicates how 'politics changes when the idea of abstract rights vocally claimed by individuals gives way to a plurality of embodied actors who enact their claims, sometimes through language and sometimes not' (Butler, 2015: 157). In this context, Rao, the feminist performer, voices and embodies the desire for 'political changes' within the assemblies. Given the absence of strong progressive movements in the present climate of neoliberalism, she has a role to play as the catalyst for radical democratic practices. All the performances of *Walk* considered here emerged out of popular demands: to end sexual violence, to be liberated from Article 377, and to resist the attack by the state. All were performed in the politically charged atmosphere of public assemblies. Ultimately, Rao's performances fostered a politicizing strategy based on hegemonizing common sense – a strategy trenchant in its opposition to the right-wing government. As that government remains in power, Rao's performance activism is firmly set to continue.

4 Performing Dissent As Citizens of Democracy

Rao's performance activism, her increasing engagement with public causes, her growing antagonism, and her expressions of dissent from the recent majoritarian communal politics require additional contextualization regarding changes in Indian politics. The right-wing BJP and its coalition, the National Democratic Alliance, won electoral victories in 2014 and 2019, gaining power and popularity through mass cultural mobilization along communal and jingoistic lines.[22] This undermined the foundations of Indian democracy that had made provision for an ecosystem of minorities by promoting divisions between the majoritarian Hindus and other minority communities, particularly Muslims. It called for renewed activism or, in the case of Rao, performance activism. Yet as the urgency for performance activism increased, sites for mass assembly were appropriated by right-wing populist forces who inflamed the communal crisis through racist and xenophobic rhetoric.

With a renewed sense of urgency, Rao and other artists sought out smaller sites in which to stage their dissent. Citizen forums such as Not in My Name (2017) and Artistes United Against Hate (2019) were formed. Rao created new performances for all the protests organized by these forums, notably protests against the attacks on Muslims that included public lynching. As Rao explains, she always tries not to refuse invitations to such events and works hard to create a performance that will resonate with and for a particular cause (Rao, 2021c).

This regressive political environment took another turn, one which this section explores: the Citizenship Amendment Act (CAA) passed by the Indian Parliament in November 2019 and the ensuing protests, particularly at Shaheen Bagh, a neighbourhood in South Delhi. Briefly, by way of introduction, the CAA, as Niraja Gopal Jayal points out, maps 'a foundational shift in the Indian conception of citizenship, providing paths to citizenship for some (favoured groups, the Hindus) while carving out statelessness for others and transforming India into a majoritarian polity' (Jayal, 2019). The CAA requires documentary proof of being an Indian on the basis that at the time of birth neither parent was an illegal migrant. Contrastingly, preferred groups – that is, religious minorities from the neighbouring Muslim majority states of Pakistan, Afghanistan, and Bangladesh – can acquire fast-track citizenship. Jayal encapsulates the major features of the CAA as moving away: from soil to blood; from *jus soli* or birth-based principles of citizenship to *jus sanguinis* as a descent-based principle of citizenship; from a religiously neutral law to a law that differentiates on the basis of religious identity and aims to render differences as a graded hierarchy; from civic nationalism to ethnic nationalism, thereby weakening the concept of political community and its terms of membership while also eroding a commitment to human rights, the moral and legal personhood of all human beings (Jayal, 2019).

Objecting to this draconian legislation, women from the Muslim community of Shaheen Bagh sat in a long durational protest from 15 December 2019 until

---

[22] Communal politics in the Indian context refers to the major communities, the Hindus and the Muslims, divided on religious lines with a long history of violence and antagonism, regarded as the cause of partitioning the country in 1947 into India, Pakistan, and what is now Bangladesh.

the outbreak of the coronavirus pandemic in early 2020. Rao was active at Shaheen Bagh in various ways as I detail shortly. Her participation included a performance at Shaheen Bagh, among the women sitting in protest, and at other spaces. Mapping where Rao performed, I aim to highlight the crisis of democracy and civil society in light of the anti-Muslim phobia unleashed by the Hindu right wing. In this context, I claim that activism, particularly performance activism, reformulated the relationships between art, life, and politics.

4.1 Performance Activism and Communal Violence

The coming to power of the BJP and Prime Minister Modi in 2014 and Modi's re-election in 2019 strengthened communal ideology that yielded an exclusionary universalism determined by the criteria of the majoritarian Hindu religion. The first phase of the right-wing attacks unsurprisingly targeted the Muslim community in India, estimated in 2019 to comprise approximately 11 per cent (204 million) of the Indian population. Muslim citizens were hounded on the flimsy pretexts of cow slaughter or for carrying or trading beef; many were publicly lynched and killed by violent mobs on the rampage, claiming to be cow-protection groups and militant Hindus, thriving on the promise of legal impunity sometimes officially, other times discreetly.[23] Shalson, analysing spectacles of public lynching in the context of the 1960s Greensboro protests in the United States, observes that these are '"dramatic" displays of racism and injustice [that] do not always inspire action against these things but frequently have served to confirm and preserve unjust racist systems', thereby reaffirming discrimination with victims 'terrorized and often immobilized into fear' (Shalson 2018: 87–8). The terrorizing of one such victim in India occurred in June 2017 as Junaid Khan, on his way home from Okhla (Delhi) to his village in Uttar Pradesh for Eid celebrations, was abducted, beaten, and killed by a group of fellow Hindu travellers who were hurling abuse at him in the name of religion. Under the banner of 'Not in My Name', artists, intellectuals, left-wing groups, and feminists came together to protest. An event was organized at Jantar Mantar on 28 June 2017 which spread to many other sites across the country.

The piece Rao created for this protest, *In the Name of the Cow* (June 2017), had two strands: one concerned naming each victim and his/her history; the other evoked the figure of Gandhi, who professed a deep love for the Muslim

---

[23] Violence on the pretext of cow slaughter and cow protection, a common occurrence in India since 2014, works as a nexus between the state, new legislations, police, and Hindu mobs (www .indiaspend.com/every-third-indian-cop-thinks-mob-violence-over-cow-slaughter-is-natural-new-survey; www.indiaspend.com/99-38-indians-now-live-in-areas-under-cow-protection-laws-42787).

community for which he paid with his life in 1948.[24] Reading from pieces of paper, Rao called out the names of each and every victim of recent times, described the brutal lynching of Khan, and ended with a call for justice. When she called out Junaid's name, her voice was full of anguish. To the accompaniment of music, she gave a speech performance which generated an atmosphere of protest and agitation while again moving her audience to think of action, to seek justice. Her constant reference to Gandhi aimed to highlight how the father of the nation was committed to communal harmony so people did not forget right-wing factions were abusing the very principles he stood for – a country of multiple religions, all living peacefully in coexistence. Overall, Rao's performance at the site constituted political dissent from the atrocities committed in the name of the Hindu majority.

The contrast between mass gatherings fuelled by right-wing populism and protests from the left and feminists became increasingly marked. On the eve of the national election in 2019, another anti-right protest was launched under the banner 'Artistes United Against Hate'. This was designed as a larger event to be held on the grounds of the historic Red Fort on 2 and 3 March 2019. However, on 14 February 2019, an incident in Pulwama (Kashmir) in which forty Indian security officers were killed by a suicide bomber, escalated tension between India and Pakistan, leading to Indian air strikes on Balakot. Jingoistic cries against Pakistan, interspersed with the rhetoric of communal hatred against Muslims in India, pervaded the country (*India Today*, 2019).[25] This jingoistic energy, garnered around an impeding war against Pakistan, fuelled support for the prime minister and his party. It can be understood in terms of what Anupama Roy describes as typical of a consensus based on religio-ethnic notions of belonging conflated with patriotism and underpinned by the fear of threats to internal or external security, ultimately leading to an acceptance of 'subordinate citizenship', particularly in relation to Muslim minorities (Roy, 2016: 173). This is in contrast to what, borrowing from James Holston, she identifies as the insurgent citizen: one who is invested in dissent in a rational space of representations where critical politics resurface and ' also emerge from a world beyond the struggles around constitutional text and its meaning, in a domain permeated by performative acts of the power of the state and people's resistance to the

---

[24] Mahatma Gandhi was assassinated on 30 January 1948 by Nathuram Godse (1910–49), who belonged to the Rashtriya Swayamsevak Sangh (National Volunteer Organization), now a sister organization of the ruling BJP.

[25] India and Pakistan were partitioned at the end of colonial rule, with Pakistan seen as the home of the Muslim populations. Aspersions are frequently cast on the Muslim population in India regarding their allegiance to Pakistan, perceived as an enemy nation, or for forging ties with terrorists in Pakistan.

exercise of such power' (Roy, 2016: 179). Rao can be regarded as a harbinger of such resistance – mobilizing insurgent citizens like herself.

Rao's performance of *Soil of Lal Qila* (2 March 2019) also called for dissent. In this piece, she drew the audience's attention to the performance site, the historic Red Fort, where Indian independence had been declared in 1947 by the first prime minister of India, Jawaharlal Nehru, and Indians became citizens of the newborn nation. It was on this site, she recalled, that Nehru raised the Indian flag, where soldiers of the Indian National Army under Netaji Subash Bose were tried and executed by the British in 1946, and where a battle for the first war of independence was fought in 1857 to oust the British and reinstate the last Mughal emperor, Bahadur Shah Zafar. She called out to the artistic Fauj (contingent), an artist's army, to fight and challenge the jingoistic and chauvinistic distortion of Indian history, particularly its anti-colonial struggle. Rao went on to expose the empty historical rhetoric to highlight the growing socio-economic disparity. Suddenly, squatting on the floor in the style of the working class in India, she said, 'I want food in my mouth', and made a poignant appeal, 'No more, not one more five years' (Figure 7). Rao's performance, against the backdrop of war cries dominating the public domain and the media, resonated with what Tony Fisher and Eve Katsouraki state should be grasped at the symbolic level, where 'social reality is seen to be discursively constructed, and where the social imaginary is constituted' (Fisher and Katsouraki, 2017: 6). In contrast to the present social reality based on communal hatred, Rao evokes a social imaginary rooted in history and the founding vision of the nation, which, Jayal argues, 'was emphatically civil-national in form' (Jayal, 2019). Rao's performance thus strongly voices how democracy in India has survived by acknowledging the plurality of socio-religious identities based on secular principles as embodied in the constitution.

Rao, along with civil society activists speaking on behalf of the Muslim community, was different to the anti-CAA protests I now move to consider. A significant difference was that the latter were led by the Muslim communities, particularly their women, thus initiating a crucial shift in who was 'authoring' the protest. Moreover, unlike the preparators of violence controlling spectacles, objectifying their victims, denying them agency and their capacity to alter the course of the events, the anti-CAA protests opposed violence and questioned the basis of the new draconian CAA. All of this led to what Shalson terms a protest-endurance perform-ance and the formation of a different role for artist-activists like Rao (Shalson, 2018).

Figure 7 *Soil of Lal Qila*: Maya Rao at Artistes United Against Hate (Photo by
Bishnupriya Dutt)

4.2 Citizenship, Protests, and Shaheen Bagh

The widespread protests against the CAA brought the hitherto invisible Muslim
community into the public domain to express dissent from members of the right
wing, who were celebrating their electoral victories and asserting that they were
the sole representative of the people, and that the civil society protests were
insignificant and not representative of the larger population.

After a particularly horrific incident at Jamia Milia Islamia University in
Delhi on 15 December 2019, when students were beaten up by the police inside
the university library and on the campus, tear-gassed, arrested, and harassed,
distressed women from the nearby area of Shaheen Bagh, who had gone to the
campus to provide support, came back and started squatting on the roads. What
started with a handful of women soon grew to unprecedented numbers. Women
joined the protest by sitting on the roads, claiming their rights as citizens, and
demanding the withdrawal of the CAA.

Shalson regards sit-ins as endurance practices. These are collectively created
by the protesters, who have '"authorship" of the scenes, even if *they [do] not*
fully control the outcome' (Shalson, 2018: 89). Hence, the sit-in can be seen as
a 'formal practice with identifiable structures at the heart of its complex and

multiple manifestations' (Shalson, 2018: 7). Rather than acting out a scripted scenario, the women at Shaheen Bagh performed simple actions according to a basic set of rules; they occupied the protest site for a full twenty-four hours each day, huddled together in woollens and blankets to ward off the cold winter; dressed in burqas, they sat, fulfilled a number of household duties like supervising children or making them do their homework, and spoke to all who came, including the media. When in need of dramatic action, they read from the constitution, 'We the People', unfolded a sixty-foot banner inscribed with the introductory statement of the Indian constitution, sang the national anthem, and raised the tricolour flag. They remained polite and passive in response to any aggression against them, stayed steadfast in their demands to repeal the CAA, and invited dialogue with the state.

Artworks, graffiti, libraries, and exhibition galleries were a feature of the site. There were two significant installations: a map of India cast in iron, and a detention camp that was a claustrophobic space. There was a tent in which the women would gather. A stage was built inside; it was very low and surrounded by photographs of nationalist leaders who stood for secularism and Hindu-Muslim unity. The site had to be expanded to accommodate the growing crowds who thronged to Shaheen Bagh. Numbers averaged between ten thousand and fifty thousand; the highest footfall was recorded as one hundred and fifty thousand on 12 January 2020 (Salam and Ausaf, 2020: xviii).[26] Overall, the site represented collective subjectivities, included artwork, songs, recitation, music, and agitprop theatre to create a liminal space between active and passive resistance in which the real and symbolic converged to create an alternative image/imagining of the nation, one resonant with Butler's notion of the enactment and assertion of popular sovereignty. According to Butler, 'Popular Sovereignty makes sense only in this perpetual act of separating from state sovereignty; thus it is a way of *forming* a people through acts of self-designation and self-gathering; these are repeated enactments, verbal and non-verbal, bodily and virtual, undertaken across different spatial and temporal zones, and on different kind of public stages, virtual realities and shadow regions' (Butler, 2015: 170). The visibility of those whom the state wanted to exclude and those who joined the protests, fighting for an ideal, conceptually highlighted an alternate value system and imagination of the 'people'. This was a political community intent on asserting popular sovereignty in defiance of state sovereignty. Shaheen Bagh inspired many other such sites in Delhi and all over India. By the end of January 2020, Delhi had twenty-two protest sites;

---

[26] On 12 January 2020, came rumors that a United Nations delegation would be visiting the site, though this was never confirmed.

others were situated in Lucknow, Allahabad, Kolkata, Bhopal, Patna, Ahmedabad, Jaipur, Bengaluru, and Chennai (Salam and Ausuaf, 2020).

Rao sat with the women from Shaheen Bagh on a daily basis, following their rules of action, revelling in the charged atmosphere, and discussing their activities (Rao, 2021d). She said for her it was 'different and new' and, in a candid moment of self-reflection, explained she had never had a friend until then who wore a burqa. Because of her regular engagement at the site, she made many 'very dear friends' (Rao, 2021d) with whom she still collaborates on her performance projects.

For activists like Rao coming from outside of the Shaheen Bagh community, getting to know the women at the heart of the protest meant understanding how they were subjected to multiple intersecting modes of discrimination – gender, class, caste, and religion. To recognize these axes of discrimination is to acknowledge what Shalson insightfully observes is the way in which socially marginalized subjects who protest also perform their 'objecthood'. Writing on a cognate protest context, she explains: 'the protesters not only demanded recognition as authorial subjects, but also engaged in a performance of object-hood that acknowledged the material conditions of existing as a body, that can be both acted upon and abandoned, that is both separate and always in relation' (Shalson, 2018: 92). This is not then to '*reject* objecthood as such, but to re-discover and reassert its inextricable connection to subjectivity as well as its central role in the *self*/other relations' (Shalson, 2018: 97).[27] In the case of the CAA protests, Rao's engagement with the women of Shaheen Bagh encouraged her to explore her own subject position: to refuse the binary logic that separates the active subject and passive object and to rethink relationality and intersub-jective desires and identifications. This is evidenced through her dialogically, rather than didactically, conceived performance of *Yeh Kya Khusboo Hai?* (*What Fragrance Is This?*) (19 January 2020).

4.3 Maya Rao in Solidarity

Performing *Yeh Kya Khusboo Hai?* Rao appeared on the makeshift stage in the women's tent. Spatially, this was a different, potentially hierarchical arrange-ment, in contrast to the way Rao had mixed with the women of Shaheen Bagh in her daily visits to the site. Yet Rao claims that the ecstatic vocal reception

---

[27] I am particularly interested in Shalson's reference to Frantz Fanon's formulation of objectifica-tion conceived in terms of postcolonial projects where 'to be objectified is thus also to be torn apart' (Fanon quoted in Shalson, 2018: 96). In postcolonial India, the process of exclusion has never been redressed. Subject formations of citizens in a new nation invoked the objectification of certain vulnerable sections of the population, particularly the Muslims, in the face of communal conflict, widespread riots, and the partition of the country at the time of independence.

throughout the performance, notably in its finale (see later in this section), elicited moments of coming together again (Rao, 2020). If there was an egalitarian relationship between artist and performance, this was because Rao's creativity stemmed from her daily immersions in the site, in contrast to other performances where she was the activist-performer invited to perform for a political cause.

While *Yeh Kya Khusboo Hai?* was deeply rooted in the political impulses circulating in Shaheen Bagh, Rao also contextualized the women's present struggles within the historical process of subject formations in postcolonial India. Turning to history, Rao deployed a Brechtian-feminist strategy of historicization through the gestic use of soil, salt, and saree. A pile of brown soil lay at her feet, signifying how the CAA had undermined *jus soli* principles of birth on the soil, representative – metaphorically and literally – as a counter to the 'documents' that were being debated as the material basis of citizenship. She trod on the soil, left her footprints, then grasped the soil in her hands and raised her fist in the air for the soil to trickle through her fingers. She referred to this as the soil of the land where all citizens belong, the soil of the country and the soil on which we have been born, grown into adults, and given birth to children and lived on the land. She declared, 'We do not need paper – we lay siege to this land.'

In a similar gesture, she picked up salt, which lay mixed with the soil, and warned the state that she and her collaborators at Shaheen Bagh would march on the soil with salt in their fists in the style of Gandhi's salt march, evoking memories of the biggest civil disobedience campaign in Indian history. Thereafter, Rao slowly changed her costume, stripping down to a blouse and petticoat, and then putting on a red saree that differentiated her from the burqa-clad Muslim women of Shaheen Bagh but gestured to the importance of solidarity. She then held up her saree as a national flag, but a blank one not marked by divisions or borders. Slowly turning around, she held the two ends of the saree to create the diamond shape of India, mapping the country as belonging to all those who inhabit it. The women around her cheered as they identified with these embodied symbolic gestures. The map, the flag, and the burqa had been symbolically deployed by the women at the site; Rao's performance gesturally and aesthetically marked their significance, amplified by the addition of citations from India's history.

Janelle Reinelt emphasizes that, in performance, 'to historicize, the incidents of [a] narrative' requires positioning 'events within a context that both explains them and yet is not necessary (i.e. it could have been otherwise)' (Reinelt, 1996: 10). All politically committed theatre, she elaborates, 'must represent the possibility of change. In order to do so it must represent the particularities of the situation in time and space, the power dynamics operating in and on the situation and the ideological formations that govern the field of discourse' (Reinelt 1996: 10). The sense that the present could be 'otherwise' is forcefully rendered in *Yeh Kya Khusboo Hai?* through Rao's strategic recourse to India's past: the history of the nation's formation symbolized in the constitution, which refers to India as a 'sovereign, socialist, secular and democratic Republic' (Preamble to the Indian constitution), or the flag which contains both saffron and green (colours historically associated with Hindus and Muslims). As politically committed theatre, the possibility of change appears in this contrast between the vision of a democratic past and a draconian present – a contrast that urges a return to humanity. As Amit Chaudhuri observed of Shaheen Bagh: 'We had forgotten what it meant to fight for humanity, because it had become blurred as an idea, or an ideal. Fighting from an ideal itself belonged conceptually to another epoch and value system' (Chaudhuri, 2020: 15).

Rao's performance culminated in a moment in which she, the map of India, slowly turned around as the music changed and strings of tied scarves, dupattas, and sarees, all previously collected from the protesting women and tied together, were thrown into the audience (Figure 8). From different corners of the tent, the women of Shaheen Bagh picked up the clothes and people who were on the periphery swelled the circle of participants who now moved to the rhythm of the beating music. As an ending it was infused with a sense of collaboration: a theatrical gesture of solidarity that was idealistic but in the moment felt very real. In this finale, everyone was interpellated as an 'insurgent citizen' (Roy, 2016: 158), capturing the idea of a political community in the making, one drafting its own new practices of democratic citizenship.

The experiences of Shaheen Bagh subsequently found their way into Rao's solo performance, *Loose Women*, staged on 15 February 2020 at the National Theatre Festival (Bharat Rang Mahotsav) (BRM). The women of Shaheen Bagh appeared on a cyclorama and a string of dupattas made waves on the screen. In the foreground, Rao hung a white saree belonging to her mother; on it she drew lines denoting borders and crossings. Rao declared, 'If you draw a line inside me, I will pull it out.' She also narrated her experiences and stories of acquaintances from Shaheen Bagh. On the saree she penned a letter to her mother.[28] Isolated, single words became visible: stain, footprints, wash, salt, and then the number 19,06,657 (the number of people identified as non-citizens because of the absence of certificates and documents). Against these words, Rao told the

---

[28] Rao tells us she inherited the saree from her mother.

Figure 8 *Yeh Kya Khusboo Hai? (What Fragrance Is This?)*: Maya Rao and her Shaheen Bagh co-actors at JNU (Photo by Samim Asgor Ali)

story of a little girl from Assam facing deportation while with her hands she performed gestures of reconciliation, solidarity, and resilience.

All told, Shaheen Bagh and the CAA protests have had a profound impact on Rao. In a conversation, she describes Shaheen Bagh as India's Floyd moment (referring to the Black Lives Matter movement in the United States) and talks about her work becoming increasingly politicized (Rao, 2021e). To understand why this should be so impactful, we have to acknowledge the capacity this long, durational protest had to forge a site of counter-hegemonic struggle as activists like Rao came out in solidarity with the women of Shaheen Bagh. The protest was politically significant in its articulation of dissent from state sovereignty. It was culturally symbolic in advocating a return to citizenship based on a 'civil-national' conception rooted in ideas of democracy and secularism, two terms the current Indian government rejects. Further, being an artist unknown to the Shaheen Bagh community and immersed in the daily life of the site yielded a different 'artivist' process for Rao than that she had previously experienced as a celebrated activist-performer invited to perform for a political cause, as was the case with her protest 'walk'. In feminist terms, this immersion in a community of vulnerable, excluded citizens afforded Rao a heightened awareness of '*self*/other relations' and an opportunity to reflect on her own subject position. Reaching different communities and publics is an enduring characteristic of Rao's career with her performance activism taking place not just on the streets but also in the theatre, as the next section details.

5 Feminist Theatre Practice and Maya Rao's Solo Performances

Thus far, the focus of this study has been on Rao's performances on the streets, from her agitprop theatre for the women's movement in the late 1970s to her performance activism in the context of neoliberalism and India's authoritarian swing to the right. However, as stated at the outset, Rao's career as a performance maker involves both the streets and the theatre. Hence, in this final main section, I turn to Rao's work in theatre spaces, bringing this firmly into view and into dialogue with her performance activism.

After their initial engagement with the Theatre Union (see Section 2), Rao and Kapur, along with several women directors, collaborated with actors, scenographers, musicians, film-makers, artists, and writers to create a significant corpus of work for dedicated theatre spaces. This body of work was radical in terms of offering a new women-oriented theatrical language and consciousness. Throughout the 1980s and 1990s, this work was generated mostly in Delhi in amateur theatres. It was staged in spaces ranging from proscenium theatres to studio theatres, art galleries, schools, colleges, and university halls. Most practitioners of the emergent women's theatre were associated with the National School of Drama as students or teachers, faculty or visiting directors in the production-oriented curriculum. Partha Chatterjee describes how, 'Keen to provide the official stamp of national modernity on various branches of cultural production, the post-colonial state created institutions such as the Sangeet Natak Akademi and the National School of Drama to extend financial, infrastructural and pedagogical support to the theatre. In the process ... the post-colonial state gave birth to the Indian National Theatre' (Chatterjee, 2016: 208) Or, as Anuradha Kapur explains, this process institutionalized an aggregate of diverse theatre practices (Kapur, 2021b). Nonetheless, feminist practices thrived and marked distinct shifts and changes from prevailing theatre practices, notably as they intervened in conventional modes of representation – mobilizing gender, experimenting with the body, and exploring a new linguistic idiom. While many directors wanted to maintain a more limiting, broad definition of women's theatre, the likes of Rao and Kapur were committed to the more radical explorations of a *feminist* theatre practice.

I begin this section by examine Rao's early work with women directors engaged in feminist practice; thereafter I look at how these collaborations enabled her to branch out into solo feminist performance, assessing this as an important contribution to feminist theatre practice in postcolonial India. Rao's solo shows are numerous and varied, but the representative performances offered here are: *Khol Do* (*Open Up*) (1993), *Ravanama* (2011), her autobiographical works *Deep Fried Jam* (2002) and *Loose Women* (2018), and, finally, her bold comedy, *The Non Stop Feel Good Show* (2011), which critiques the media and its promotion of women as consumers of the health and beauty industries in twenty-first-century, neoliberal India. In analysing Rao's solo work, I address the contradiction between the notion of the solo performer as an authorial presence (Jestrovic, 2020) and Rao's enactment of multiple personas and her recourse to collaboration. Further, I touch on the critique of feminist theatre practice in an Indian context: the accusation that it is exclusive, middle class, and urban in orientation, entrenched in social and cultural capital. A. Mangai in *Acting Up* (2015) explains there is an 'unresolved contradiction between feminist political action and feminist theatre', urging that this should be considered as a 'feminist continuum' (Mangai, 2015: 35). However, in what follows, I posit the move into institutional spaces or the proscenium stage as much of a break as a continuity.

5.1 Locating and Identifying Feminist Theatre

In her seminal essay 'Reassembling the Modern: An Indian Theatre Map since Independence' (2009), Kapur elaborates on common trajectories across the theatre of women directors such as Amal Allana, Anamika Haksar, Neelam Mansingh Chawdhry, herself, and Rao. She argues that this corpus of work created a radical break from the earlier postcolonial nation-building projects of Indian theatre that did not address subjectivities or gender. She summarizes the theatre of her contemporaries as initiating radical dramaturgical interventions through the processes of directing or constructing the play, emphasizing the collective, and a mode of collaboration between director and performers. Dramatic events were no longer the domain of 'heroic actions' but took the form of fragmented moments illuminating ordinary activities; dramatic structures were non-linear, refusing resolution and closure; plot/character configurations moved towards 'a new set of subjectivities in order to unsettle expected portrayals' (Kapur, 2009: 50–1). Unlike agitprop deployed for feminist campaigns, where the realities of suffering women had to be at the centre (Section 2), working in dedicated theatre spaces allowed for the radical possibilities of mobilizing gender through a new range of theatrical strategies such as masquerade, androgyny, multiple identities, and subjectivities 'crossing society's artificially maintained boundaries of roles and stations; objects can induce relationships, and imaginary landscapes produce tangible attachments' (Kapur, 2009: 51).

Kapur's overview identifies the collaboration between actor and director as core to this practice. Rao worked with several women directors as an actor-collaborator, performing in some of the landmark productions that were foundational to an emergent feminist-theatre practice. Under Kapur's direction, she performed in Brecht's *Mother* (adapted from Maxim Gorki's 1906 novel of the same name) and *St. Joan of the Stockyard* (1971). Both were staged in a Brechtian mode in order to examine the material conditions of gender behaviour. Subsequently, Rao worked with Amal Allana and Anamika Haksar. Allana trained in the erstwhile German Democratic Republic in the Brechtian method (later also in a Japanese performance genre). Haksar trained at the State Institution of Theatre Arts in Moscow. Rao herself trained at Leeds University and Leeds Playhouse TIE Company in the United Kingdom. These different training methods invoked a socialist ethos that endorsed a democratic approach to rehearsals and acting methods, thereby dismantling conventional theatrical hierarchies.

Allana collaborated with Rao as early as 1980 on the *House of Bernarda Alba* (translated as *Birjees Qadar ka Kunba* (*The Family/Clan of Birjees Qadar*)) and later in 1989 on a magnum opus of *King Lear*. Allana's working process entailed building an ensemble and, in *Bernarda Alba*, she worked with an all-women cast. The long rehearsal process and the days spent on improvisation fostered an intimacy and an openness that led to exchanging ideas and expressing uninhibited bodily proximity and touch. Rao as Poncia, Allana says, was the counterpoint to the matriarch, Bernarda, who had assumed the mantle of the dead patriarch. Poncia embodied earthiness, raw sexuality, and raunchiness, which Rao instinctively manifested through bodily impulses (Allana, 2021). Allana works on elaborate rehearsal processes in which, she explains, she often sits back and allows her actors to construct roles and scenes, from outside with surface details as well as with internalization. She lets the outcome of this improvisation process by the actors become the performance text, even if it means altering the dramatic textual source; ideally, this process results in a transition from showing to becoming. She says, 'I am interested in the persona of the Actor, his/her journey both by what one does and a theme he/she wishes to explore, these are not different processes but part of the same process' (Allana, 2021). In *Lear*, Rao played Goneril; it was a production where elements of Kathakali – expansive postures, big gestures, large costumes, and headwear – were adapted to create a spatial presence for the actors, who performed outdoors in a space of half an acre in the Pragati Maidan. Rao worked with Allana on the choreography and training.

Haksar adapted her own Moscow-based training to engage in lengthy processes that encouraged performers to enlarge their worlds. She explains her belief that what is core to Stanislavski's method is the much-misunderstood concept of 'Dusha' – the soul – compelling one to take stimulus from the world at large but also exploring the subconscious with an internal focus, thereby creating a unique language made manifest in both psychological and physical traits (Haksar, 2018). On her return from the USSR, Haksar directed a production based on Gogol's *Viy* (1988), a novelette of magic and grotesque realism. For this she used elaborate stylized movements from Kathakali and Chhau as well as psychological intensity. Rao played the lead female role, a witch who is also a beautiful woman. She rides on the shoulders of a young student, Khoma Brut, to show him a different perspective on the world from that constrained by the closed walls of the monastery where he studies and lives. The stage depicted a church vault seen through a monolithic arch and long, stained-glass windows featuring iconography of the Orthodox Church; it opened up to reveal the expanded space of the church as a metaphor for the exterior world.[29] The external landscape was shown through Rao's body and eyes. Ravindra Sahu as Khoma Brut was guided by her as he traversed the wild landscape of nature – a dreamscape imagined purely in the eyes of the actors and through their tensed bodies. In the final scene, Rao appeared to expand into nature: costumed in green and joined by other women also in green, she ripped open the church to merge with the natural landscape. Kapur, in characterizing Haksar's work, reads this as an 'interjection of the self into a landscape and desire, (where) thought and longing are made visibly manifest' (Kapur, 2009: 54–5).

This brief overview of emergent feminist-theatre practices in India confirms the centrality of Rao to their emergence and development. In turn, being a part of this new feminist landscape in Indian theatre enabled Rao to transition into solo work. In many ways, her turn to solo performance involved a more radical adaptation of the main features of feminist practices as defined by Kapur – events broken into moments, each improvised; no semblance of plots or narrative strategies even when derived from important short stories or the epic *Ramayana* (see Section 5.2); and characters presented as multiple rather than singular entities In particular, Rao's emergent work as a solo performer brought what Kapur, Allana and Haksar, and Rao's own training encouraged actors to explore: split subjectivities and various personas of the artistic self. In short, as the performer and performance maker in her solo pieces, Rao found the freedom to expand her experimentation into new feminist idioms and aesthetics, an experimentation that also saw her moving towards androgyny. Drawing on autobiographical experiences or impulses, she invented multiple personas designed to question social and political roles and identities and to explore the discursive in a dialectical relationship between herself and the roles she played. Formally, this new solo work was underpinned by her training and proficiency in Kathakali; this would become the dominant form from which Rao sourced her gendered vocabulary. Kathakali requires not only years of training, but also

---

[29] The church interior was designed by the architect Ranesh Ray and the painter Sumantra Sen.

an individualistic interpretation of characters and roles; it typically favours a solo endeavour on the part of the dancer-actor. If, in one way, Rao's move into solo work can be seen as a continuation or expansion of new feminist theatre practices, in another it marks a significant break. Going solo necessitated a departure from the founding, feminist-theatre principle of collaboration. No longer working in collaboration with a director and actors, Rao was now the sole/solo author and performer.

5.2 Narrating Stories from History and the Epics

Rao devised and performed her first solo piece, *Khol Do*, in 1993, which she describes as a dance-theatre work based on Sadat Hasan Manto's short story about a father's search for his daughter lost amidst the large-scale migrations and communal riots between India and Pakistan at the time of partition in 1947. In this non-verbal short piece, Rao appears as both the father and the daughter. It opens with Rao, dressed in white pyjamas and a shirt, lying inert at the centre of the stage, like a corpse. Slowly, her body begins to stir, her legs moving in the air, flailing, as the father, Sirajuddin, struggles to rouse his body and gain consciousness. While crossing the border in a train between India and Pakistan, he has been assaulted by a mob of rioters, His wife has been killed and his daughter, Sakina, has gone missing. In the ten-minute opening sequence, Rao attempts to rise from the inertia caused by the trauma. Slowly gaining strength and consciousness, she stands up with her arms in the air and with a roar raises her arms against the shrill soundtrack of a passing train, trying to stop it, and turns around as she is silhouetted against a red light.

Arousing himself from the stupor, Sirajuddin starts a desperate search for his daughter. In his memories, a child's laughter is heard. Rao plays the child, crawling and circling the stage and playing games. She takes off three white bangles from her wrist and spreads them on the floor and plays with them, clapping in childlike delight, occasionally transforming into the father, who holds the child in the crook of his arm. This sequence is interrupted by sounds of a train. Rao shifts to depict the horror of rape that has befallen Sakina. Her Kathakali-styled facial expressions depict delight, changing to terror (Figure 9). Slowly, she covers her face and collapses, picking up a blue scarf lying on the ground and intertwines it around her body; she lets it fall over her leg, covers her vagina, and drags it across her body to end as a gag across her mouth. This anticipates Sirajuddin's actual discovery of what happened to his daughter: the inert Sakina opens the strings of her pyjamas, indicating that she, like millions of other women, had been violated and raped as hate and venom flooded the country. Rao clutches the scarf, writhing in agony. But slowly she gets up,

Figure 9 *Khol Do*: Maya Rao as Sirajuddin and Sakina, in a Kathakali pose
(Photo by S. Thyagarajan/National School of Drama archives)

shedding off the pain. She sits nonchalantly, facing the right, straightening her blue scarf as she looks sideways into the audience. Her expression is poignant; her eyes seep unbearable pain. She holds this expression as the lights dim. It seems as though she is looking out of a window onto a new world, the birth of a nation marked by violence against women.

In her solo shows, Rao rarely works from an established text. Beyond *Khol Do* is one important exception: her adaptation of the epic *Ramayana* titled *Ravanama*.[30] This is the story of the anti-hero, Rama's enemy, Ravana, a popular deviation in the Kathakali repertoire which M. Narayanan regards as the ascent of the anti-heroic character in what is an essentially heroic form, played as a celebration of arrogant power and defiance (Narayanan, 2010: 1–2). Rao says that her starting point was the celebrated piece from the Kathakali repertoire where Ravana holds the stage for more than an hour (Rao, 2021b).

---

[30] Rao first performed *Ravanama* as part of a seminar and performance festival on Ramayana organized by Adhishakti in Pondicherry in 2011.

As far as epics are concerned, numerous versions try to depict Ravana's redeeming qualities, and Rao devised one such version that portrayed Sita as his lost daughter. Thus, like *Khol Do*, the focus is on father-daughter relations. That said, there is no conventional portrayal of fathers and daughters. Rather, Rao reinvents and presents these roles as personas of the artist in a way that allows her to interrogate patriarchy. In *Ravanama*, she plays both Ravana and Sita and performs 'herself' as she searches newspapers and her laptop, exploring how to represent the story in a way that displaces familiar narratives and characterizations. Ultimately, Rao's intervention into the epic, often depicted as a sacrosanct text for Hindus, is radical: it is no longer a story of revenge by the hero Rama, but an amalgamation of local myths, folk performances, and popular renderings which comprise counter narratives told from the perspectives of the anti-hero and the woman protagonist.

Although derived from canonical sources, the storylines in both *Khol Do* and *Ravanama* serve as mere impulses or catalysts for Rao's devising (a strategy also evident in her radical rendition of Shakespeare's *Macbeth*, as touched on in Section 1). Rao's dramaturgical reworkings of these canonical texts depends on an intense working process. Each moment she devises is packed with many layers that involve moving effortlessly between speech, stylized gestures, intense movements, pure dance, expressions through the face and eyes, and occasional moments of realism. Her Kathakali training is drawn on extensively in her improvisations and interpretations. Rao deploys techniques from this tradition in diverse ways – to demonstrate emotion, to embody and enact a narrative sequence, or to hybridize with other performance registers (Figure 10). In contrast to the physicality and gestural movements such techniques require, Rao also creates moments of charged stillness and then delivers lines in accord with the realist tradition.

As both the author and performer rewriting canonical texts from the perspective of both male and female protagonists, Rao emerges as a significant 'authorial presence' (Jestrovic, 2020: 9). This runs the risk of what Silvija Jestrovic argues as 'fixity – a stable source from whom it all began and to whom there has been a longing to return in the quest for "true" meaning – the "authentic" intention' (Jestrovic, 2020: 11). Paradoxically, the more Rao deconstructs an established text, the greater her 'authorial presence' is felt: she is the 'stable source' from which meaning flows. That said, as the 'source', Rao is not quite so fixed or 'stable' as an exploration of her autobiographical solo shows demonstrates.

5.3 Solo Shows and the Performer

Rao's first autobiographical performance was *A Deep Fried Jam* in 2002. This show was a watershed: it marked the moment when Rao decided to devise from

Figure 10 *Ravanama*: Maya Rao dancing in Kathakali style to Michael Jackson's 'I am Bad' (Photo by S. Thyagarajan/National School of Drama archives)

her own life experiences.[31] Other versions of *A Deep Fried Jam* would follow over the years, including *A Deeper Fried Jam* and the latest version, *Loose Woman* (2018), a modification of the original, touching on similar themes but updated to acknowledge the passage of time. This work takes the form of a one-woman monologue, interspersed with music, dance, movement, and video projections. The content is a mix of autobiographical fragments and historical and contemporary reflections. Episodes are loosely woven together and the show plays for an hour to an hour and half. The timing is affected by audience interactions: Rao strikes up conversations (often humorous ones) with her audiences. The main focus is on her own experiences as a woman and a feminist. These she draws on to unsettle gender norms; masculinity and femininity are always referred to or played as artificial constructs. While the deconstruction of gender norms is not a new feature of Rao's work, honing her critique of gender in the autobiographical performance has proved seminal to establishing and generically defining feminist solo performance in India.

Gabrielle Griffin, writing on the British performer Clair Dowie's solo shows, argues that through the split between the solo artist's performing and performed self, the artist can trouble and unsettle identities. She explains that 'the subject

---

[31] After *Khol Do* in 1993 and prior to her departure into autobiographical work in 2002, Rao created and performed other solo shows that include *Departures* (1999), *4-Wheel-Drive-'Come-to-Me-Mr. Sharma'- Body-Fat-Murdered-Show* (1998), and *The Job* (1997), based on a short story by Bertolt Brecht.

of performance, the "I" – and the performed self – the object of the performance, the "me" . . . are both sustained and subverted by the metadiscourse through which the performing self discusses the performed self' (Griffin, 2004: 155). This serves to elucidate how Rao, working on autobiographical material, maintains a split between the present performing self and the 'me' constructed out of past autobiographical experience. Griffin adds a third dimension: 'the referent, the actual person towards whom the performing and performed selves seem to gesture' and who exists 'outside performed time' (Griffin, 2004: 156). The latter 'eludes us even as we seek to solidify it into a source of meaning' (Griffin, 2004: 156), and yet it prompts me to think of how Rao, the 'actual person', slips in and out of 'performed time' as the real-life woman who embodies and gestures to a history of feminist performance activism.

Further, on the issue of the real-life self, Jestrovic, referencing Svetlana Boym, explains that 'both the real-life self and the authorial self are etymologically related to the Latin word "persona" – meaning theatrical mask' and various degrees of self-dramatization. She points out that 'persona encompasses different kinds of disguises as it dramatizes the somebody/nobody dialectic both etymologically and performatively' (Jestrovic, 2020: 15–16). Thus, the notion of personas also assists in understanding the slippage between the real-life persona of Rao and the personas she creates and performs out of personal anecdotes and experiences. These include aspects of her life: growing up in Delhi (though she and her family came from Kerala), her father's early demise, her actress mother, and her own experience in the performing arts such as Kathakali training and college theatre, and later agitprop. These anecdotes always foreground gender; all are enacted with humour, irony, and self-deprecation, and they somehow gesture to the real-life woman behind the multiple personas.

Where father-daughter relations dominate her adaptations of canonical works, in her autobiographical performances, it is the mother who is prominent: Rao claims a matrilineal identity as the daughter of an artist mother who encouraged her to perform and to learn dance at the International Kathakali Centre and commanded her to sing, though she herself could not sing a right note and neither can Rao. When I saw *Loose Woman* performed at the Bharat Rang Mahotsav on 15 February 2020, Rao announced it was her mother's ninety-sixth birthday. No two days with her are the same, she delighted in telling the audience. She expounded upon how her mother constantly changes things in her garden and in her life. It is her mother, she tells us, who encouraged her to walk properly and to run. Rao practices the perfect walk according to her mother's instructions, which is 'not as easy as it looks'. And, when she does get a feel for how to walk a straight and/or narrow path, she learns how to side-step

Figure 11 *Loose Woman*: Learning how to side-step (Photo by S. Thyagarajan/ National School of Drama archives)

(Figure 11). Thus, she gestures to the rebel 'me': not abiding by social norms that constrain women's lives, particularly women involved in activism and the field of theatre, dance, and traditional performances.

After independence, modern Indian performing arts projects were oriented towards the reconstruction of what were to be classified and exhibited as classical Indian dances, where women artists had to display ideals of purity. In *A Deep Fried Jam* and *Loose Woman*, Rao devotes an entire episode to a humorous subversion of reconstructed classical dance and her own involve-ment in learning Kathakali as a young performer, a form that, as previously noted, she would later use to deconstruct gender norms. In this episode, she declares herself a 'dancer' and performs dance gestures: water flowing, flowers (particularly the lotus), and the bee hovering over the flowers. Technically perfect in her execution of graceful finger gestures, she undercuts them with verbal prompts, descriptions, and questions laced with sarcasm to show how literal the translations are and how these are coded as stable signs. She says, 'If

I linked one finger to the other, would it say something to you? If I held my hand as a lotus and a bee, would it?' As the bee on the flower, she lapses into representing the bee with her eye, reminiscent of Kathakali eye gestures, rendering them grotesque and breaking the feminine grace, all while her hands maintain the graceful gesture of the lotus. Inherent in her questioning is: What do such classical forms and techniques do to/for your identity? Does it make you an Indian performer, or are you performing the Indian classical dance? In *Loose Woman*, she asks, 'Did it make any sense to you?' In performing and discarding such formal gestures, Rao challenges and disrupts the stable signs of femininity in dominant cultural practices.

By 2002, India was also being heavily influenced by Western culture, courtesy of globalization and neoliberalism. Rao's title *A Deep Fried Jam* gestures to the hybrid influences of Indian tradition and Western cultural imports – upbeat blues, rap, pop, and rock music. A live band accompanies Rao on stage, provides background music, and sings and jams. In one episode, Rao sprawls diagonally on the floor, moving towards a wooden doll that stands in a corner. The doll is a traditional wooden doll dressed as a dancer, and her posture and gestures depict the classical dancing body. Rao, singing 'Oh my baby' and 'She is my girl', writhes towards her, highlighting the incongruity of Indian cultures that eulogize tradition and Western imports. In *Loose Woman*, the doll returns, positioned on the stage but also projected on a screen against the background of a busy street. Rao now walks down a ramp, singing 'Oh my baby', picking up the doll with affection, kissing and touching her, and whispering in her ears, 'After all we chose the right country, we get to sleep on the streets now,' making a reference to the scrapping of Article 377 and the Shaheen Bagh women's protests. As Rao interacts with the doll, what becomes visible is India as country that has lost its way, a country where people sleep on streets and footpaths while expensive cars jam the roads of metropolitan cities. Rao emphasizes that, in February 2020, it was a clear reference to how women had taken over the streets in Shaheen Bagh and elsewhere across the country (Section 4) (Rao, 2021b).

From *A Deep Fried Jam* to *Loose Woman*, Rao's solo performances look critically back at the 'me' that was formed through both her private and professional lives, an autobiographical exploration set against the backdrop of the nation. The period between the two versions of the show spans nearly two decades, and the rapid changes the country has undergone are evident, as exemplified by the idea of an India 'jammed' between traditional and Western cultures, endorsing a consumer culture while structural inequalities persist and escalate.

Feminist performances in India have worked extensively with properties like sand, water, and soil to represent the material realities of the nation; *A Deep Fried Jam* and *Loose Woman* follow in this tradition. For long episodes in *A Deep Fried Jam*, Rao talks of walking and running on the sand and asks, 'Will we leave a footprint on the sand, would we?' She drops a bangle on the floor and continues, 'If my foot was my pen, and my hand the ink in the pen, if we wrote our own story, round and round, would we make a mark, have a stamp?' The sand is reminiscent of the grime and dirt of the streets, but it also references the nation's history and Gandhi's salt march, a trenchant reminder of a country now failing to care for its vulnerable citizens. Rao builds a mound of sand, pours water down the crevices, and lies down to create an outline of her body. In the final episode, she covers the stage with the sand, on which light falls to create the effect of ripples on the sea. In *Loose Woman*, Gandhi's salt march reappears, but she depicts it with her hands and fingers and knotted white thread, magnified on the screen.[32] Rao, as the author-performer leaving her foot-, hand-, or body-print on the nation's soil/land, resonates with what Jestrovic calls the resurrection of the author through embodiment and mimesis (Jestrovic, 2020: 12): it is as if Rao is in a search of her own identity, sifting through the 'meta layers of narrative and theatricality' (Jestrovic, 2020: 15).

Whilst not wishing to detract from the importance of Rao's pioneering of a feminist solo performance practice in India and its deconstruction of gender norms, I need to address a criticism here, especially with regard to the 'self-centred' focus of the autobiographical work. This pertains to Rao's privileged position. Performing gender disruptions has never threatened her cultural position and stature in the theatre establishment. Neither has her citizenship been at risk, as she is a member of a cosmopolitan, cultural elite. Thus, any autobiographical quest to rediscover or seek out an 'authentic' self is marked and limited by class, by her social and cultural capital. In other words, there is a social gap between Rao 'being troubled by one's own identity' (Griffin, 2004: 153) and all those who do not share the same privilege. Ultimately, this limits the potential for the autobiographically derived solo work to achieve a more socially inclusive feminist imagination. However, this limitation is one that Rao seeks to redress in her feminist political cabaret, *Non Stop Feel Good Show*, a performance that eschews the avant-garde or experimental in favour of popular political theatre with a wide audience appeal.

---

[32] The yarn used in the performance was spun by children of the Sevagram School, started by Gandhi, that was gifted to Rao (Rao, correspondence, April 2022).

5.4 To Start Feeling Good Is to Feel Bad

In *Non Stop Feel Good Show*, created in 2011, Rao retains an autobiographical element but subjects it to a comedic critique.[33] She also broadens the content of the piece to launch an attack on the media and a culture of consumption. The show hinges on two main personas. The first is a caricature of Rao's Kerala origins. On first sight, she appears unrecognizable, bundled in a *mundu veshti* with her head covered with white marks – typical of women from Kerala – on her forehead and wearing spectacles (Figure 12).[34] The second is Rao's personification of an ultra-modern television show host in contemporary India who is intent on instructing viewers how to live a stress-free life and achieve self-improvement through cooking and fitness regimes.

Through the regional Kerala persona, she tells us the story of her 'artist' family as performers and con artists. It begins with the story of her grandparents, how they met and married and played in local theatres. This ends with the introduction of her dancer mother before she was married, when she was part of an Indian delegation to the United Nations, purportedly to showcase the country's cultural heritage.

Figure 12 *Non Stop Feel Good Show*: Maya Rao as the woman from Kerala narrating her life story (Photo by S. Thyagarajan/National School of Drama archives)

---

[33] The *Non Stop Feel Good Show* is a remodelled and updated version of *4-Wheel-Drive- 'Come-to-Me- Mr. Sharma'- Body-Fat-Murdered* (1998).

[34] Garment worn by women in Kerala: a white cloth wrapped around the waist and a matching cloth draped across the upper body.

The next part is about her mother and her con man of a father who makes them destitute, forcing her mother to become a street dancer and then a night club entertainer to feed her two children. The mother is arrested when authorities discover that the father, pretending to be an innocent fisherman, smuggles diamonds in his fishing boat. The third and final part tells her own story about how she earns money by offering elephant rides to children and driving an auto-rickshaw. A foray into the smuggling business brings her notoriety, but also prosperity and power. She runs for elections and becomes a minister – the culture minister – but is arrested and serves a term in prison from where she dances her way out. She emerges as the new don; her face appears on screen with a wicked smile: 'A Doness'.

As this brief description reveals, this section of the show transforms recognizable traits of Kerala society, where matriarchy still prevails in certain social practices, into a narrative (delivered in a strong Malayalam accent) that is increasingly absurd and fantasy laden. It is not completely divorced from reality, as Rao reminds us through the photographs that accompany the narration. These are photographs of people bearing a strong family resemblance to Rao, although, as she doodles on the images, they too turn into caricatures. This caricaturing resonates with the overall thrust of this theme of the show: the systematic displacement of Rao's familial, social, and cultural locations through self-deprecating humour and comic subversion. The absurd 'me' Rao constructs is core to that displacement, yet we still recognize her through the 'authorial presence' of her 'performing self' who constructs, authenticates the fake autobiography.

In the other part of the show, Rao switches to the persona of the television host to satirize the rise of a neoliberal culture of conspicuous consumption. Dressed in various outlandish costumes – short skirts, tight and revealing tops, a slinky black dress, or white sports apparel – she appears both ridiculous and somehow attractive. She delights in pointing out the misfit between a tight outfit and the tyres of fat across her stomach, or her sagging arms. Instructing people how to escape the stress of city living, she speaks in accented Indian English with a smattering of Hindi words. Her tips include how to avoid the stress of driving the new brands of international cars through the congested city. She talks mischievously about the Jaguar and the jogging seat it offers for health benefits. Wearing boxer shorts or a short skirt so her legs are revealed, she turns to tell her husband, who is supposedly sitting in the backseat and who rolls on her every night, that sometimes it is necessary to ask her if she is ready or is in the mood for sex. She repeatedly equates women's body parts with the parts of a car – their engines, valves, exhalation-inhalation techniques, the black body of the Opel Astra with black heads to get rid of, and metallic car colours with nail polish. Cucumbers are recommended for keeping between the thighs while driving and waiting in traffic jams. This interchange of women and cars constitutes what Elin Diamond describes as the 'phantasmagoria of industrial commodities': the 'powerful wish image of commodity culture' that is dialectical and contradictory, being exciting as a 'commodity but also a fetish and fossil, wish image and ruin' (Diamond, 1997: 178). As Diamond explains, this 'shouts volumes about sexism, ageism, youth worship, and the degradation of female experience in capitalist culture' (177).

The *Non Stop Feel Good Show* was commissioned by the Park hotel chain that belongs to an industrial house, but this did not stop Rao from biting the hand that fed her. Another episode saw her playing a cookery show host, wearing a slinky black dress that stopped above the knees, her white hair flowing and tied back with a red band. She oozed sexuality while fondling a fish, her graceful fingers rubbing its back, supposedly with olive oil and spices (Figure 13). At one point, she says, 'If you are on the fast track, thin, slim, fast, export, go for Gujrat,' which was where Narendra Modi was the chief minister. His prime-ministerial aspirations were already clear to the audience. 'In seven days time you will get land, water, electricity – a shining recipe. It doesn't matter that the national average of labour wages in Gujrat is Rs 270, compared to Rs 332, in the rest of India, but that is to your benefit.' Rao's 'recipe' for neoliberalism included abject labour conditions, poor healthcare, poverty, pollution, and the corruption that surrounds coal-rich states. All of these were 'dished up' to

Figure 13 *Non Stop Feel Good Show*: Maya Rao as the cookery show host
(Photo by S. Thyagarajan/National School of Drama archives)

audiences who evinced a healthy appetite for her savagely comedic critique of neoliberalism, palpable in the roars of laughter that greeted her political satire. Serving up her own body (the cooking ends with Rao climbing up onto the table to lie down on the fish) in the mix of this wide-ranging attack on capitalism, economic exploitation, political conservatism and rampant corruption, Rao gestures to feminism not as 'an identity category to be claimed', but, as Elaine Aston and Geraldine Harris describe, as 'a *politics* concerned with changing "things"' (Aston and Harris, 2013: 8).

After being staged on the five-star hotel circuit, in 2013, the *Non Stop Feel Good Show* appeared at the Bharat Rang Mahotsav (BRM), held at the National School of Drama. This saw Rao, an older feminist-activist performer, playing to a younger generation of women. With its accessible, popular political form and content concerning women's commodification, as well as the detrimental impact of neoliberalism at large, it proved intergenerationally successful (audiences thronged to see the performance). Urging the issue of commodification to younger women, Rao closed the show with a final, gestically rendered critique of commercialized femininity. Wearing a white dress and jacket and holding a melon, she continued to promote beauty regimes. Squeezing the juice of the melon over her head, she stained the white dress; it was almost like blood appearing. She then began to 'walk' and in that moment her solo theatre work joined her performance activism from the streets. Together they proclaimed the urgent, feminist need for 'things' to change.

Socially progressive change in India remains elusive given the country's swing to the right under Modi's prime-ministerial tenure. This has had a detrimental impact on feminism at large and in the theatre where the space for feminist work has diminished. That feminist-theatre practices manage to survive is due in no small measure to Rao. As this section has shown, Rao's transition from a seminal figure in the early beginnings of feminist theatre in India to a solo performer constituted a break with the emergent mode of collaborative, ensemble-based feminist performance. That said, continuity was found in her adherence to theatrical experimentation in and through which the performer's body was core to mobilizing an awareness of gender constructs and subjectivities, thereby expanding feminist practices through the solo performance genre. Her solo work is not without criticism, as noted in the case of the autobiographical performances where questions of privilege, urban preoccupation, and individualism arise, mirroring concerns often levelled at the feminist movement. In the final analysis, however, what is exceptional about Rao as a performance maker is the way in which she has enriched the field of Indian feminist-theatre practices *and* feminist-performance activism on the streets.

6 Conclusion

Rao's dual commitment to feminism on the streets and in the theatre distinguishes her career. This defining feature can be traced back to her agitprop beginnings when she collaborated with Kapur on the feminist campaigns to end dowry deaths and sexual violence (Section 2). The feminist movement also impacted theatre: an increasing number of women practitioners sought to make a feminist difference to conventional theatre practices. Opening *Feminist Futures?* Aston and Harris cite Sue-Ellen Case on the 'radical ways in which feminism has affected all aspects of theatre, changing theatre history and becoming a major element in twentieth-century theatre practice. The feminist critic or practitioner needs no longer adopt a polemic posture in this art, but can rely on the established feminist tradition in the theatre, with its growing number of practitioners and adherents' (quoted in Aston and Harris, 2007: 1). In an Indian context, Rao featured prominently among those women practitioners who founded a 'feminist tradition', engaging in experimental, feminist theatre practices that she subsequently pursued in her turn to the solo genre (Section 5). When she returned to street theatre and performance activism in 2012, her solo-based theatre meant she had an enriched feminist performance language through which to respond to urgent issues such as sexual violence in *Walk* (Section 3) and, thereafter, to perform dissent from the undemocratic practices of an increasingly right-wing nation (Section 4).

Performing feminism in theatres and on the streets, Rao can reach different audiences, different communities. Reinelt would argue this is the unfolding of a critical dialogue between different publics, countering the criticism that the performing arts are marginal to the 'political' (Rai and Reinelt, 2015: 34). This gestures to the important role performers can play by bringing different groups together in solidarity. Elsewhere, Reinelt elaborates that, while theatre has a more limited circulation, its staging of contemporary issues contributes 'to a public dialogue' through its '"re-characterization" and even occasional "transformation" of accounts of events circulating in the contemporary public sphere' (Reinelt 2012, 15–16). Where Rao's address of feminist issues through her solo performances can thus be understood as participating in a 'public dialogue', this is only one dialogue among the many she creates through her performance activism in non-theatre sites. Thus, overall, the 'political' claims that can be made for Rao's feminist theatre/performance activism reside in the different 'publics' she creates and is able to reach. It takes a particular kind of artistic stamina and political commitment to form these 'publics', and performing dissent from India's increasingly authoritarian regime also involves a degree of personal risk. But Rao's dedication to an Indian nation forged in the spirit of democracy remains steadfast. Through her feminist theatre, she works tirelessly and relentlessly to foster opposition to the anti-democratic landscape that now contours contemporary India.

6.1 Pandemic Postscript

Not even the coronavirus pandemic has prevented Rao from her performance-making or her activism. In November 2020, when farmers were protesting on the borders of Delhi against agricultural laws intended to promote the privatization of agriculture, Rao joined them with a piece titled *Naam Hai Aurat* (*The Name Is Woman*).[35] She performed this on Women Farmers' Day, 18 January 2021, to a large audience of women. The performance contained residual elements of earlier work. The 'soil' from Shaheen Bagh resurfaced in relation to farming and the women who had left behind their work at home and in the fields to knock on the door of the prime minister, who refused to heed their pleas. Rao praised them for their resilience and courage, but also urged them to continue and intensify affirmative actions against the state until such time as the laws were repealed. As she asked them to raise their hands to show Mr Modi the hands of the women who work the soil of India, hundreds of hands went up into the air.[36]

She also made online videos: *Lockdown Stories* (April 2020 onwards). These are short pieces revolving around a woman, Paru from Kerala, who first appeared in the *Non Stop Feel Good Show*. However, she has been transformed into an icon and appears in a series of animated photographs. Rao's voice resounds against the images, recalling the devastating conditions of the pandemic, particularly the unprecedented reverse migration, when an estimated 60–70 per cent of the labour force in Delhi left to find their way home (*Hindustan Times*, 2 June 2020). In the absence of transport, which was suddenly suspended because of the lockdown, migrant labourers walked through the vast expanse of the subcontinent, facing unprecedented hardships, some dying along the way. Rao uses a narrative style replete with biting humour, everyday wisdom, and innocence. Speaking in conversational tones and with a southern accent, she talks about the authoritative way the administration dealt

---

[35] Recent laws in the industrial and agricultural sectors abolished protective measures for workers and farmers. They are couched in neoliberal language and adopt a sledgehammer approach. Two and a half million workers went on strike on 26 November 2020, and farmers, mainly from Punjab and Haryana, marched in protest to the capital. They set up camps along key borders such as Singur, Tikri, and Ghaziabad. The farmers' protests continued for a year, until 19 November 2021, when the prime minister announced a repeal.

[36] The farmers' protests had a vibrant women's presence as exemplified by the Women Farmers' Day protest on 18 January 2021, for which mock parliamentary sessions were held while Parliament was in session to debate the agricultural laws (*Hindustan Times*: 2021).

with COVID-19 – uncaring and ruthless – while an animated heart appears on the screen with the title 'I care' (Lockdown Stories I).

She depicts the plight of the workers and migrants, explains how she (Paru) tried to make her way home to Kerala but lost her way, disoriented and in despair. Rao also calls attention to the plight of economically vulnerable women who lost their jobs and were increasingly subjected to domestic violence. When Paru's husband has COVID-19 symptoms, she sleeps in her PPE kit. A picture of Paru, huddled, wrapped up, unglamorous, and sleeping in her PPE jacket is shown, while Rao consoles her audience that it is like wearing nightclothes.

In contrast to *Lockdown I*, *Lockdown II* shuns humour. It consists of a series of short videos that, in addition to the plight of the migrant workers struggling to go back home, invokes memories of recent (pre-COVID-19) protests. The repression by the state that followed these protests coincided with the lockdown; activists were arrested and incarcerated without trials. Rao cites 'More than 800 picked up from their homes' and lists their names: Safoora Zargar, Gulfisha Fatima, Natasha Narwal, Devangana Kalita, Ishrat Jahan, Farhan Zuberi, Sharjeel Imam ... '.[37] These are the names of young activists – the university students who participated in activism and, when protests against the CAA took place, came out in solidarity with the women at the sit-ins, taking on various responsibilities to help keep the protest site going.[38] In brief, these young activists tried to ensure that the politicizing energies of the protests did not dissipate, but rather continued, if not intensified, thus giving rise to sites of counter-hegemonic struggle in and through which solidarities and collective identities could be forged and maintained.

In solidarity with the activists in prison, Rao, the performer-activist, continues to agitate and fight for justice. I give the final word to Rao, lines taken from her June 2021 video *Can't Breathe, Will Speak* (June 2021):[39]

> Yes, when I was born into this world
> I breathed – you locked the air in my throat
> With every fibre in my body
> With every gasp of breath, I speak out loud.
> You made prison walls outside of the prison?
> Locked the air, locked the air – call this freedom?
> The freedom to die in bed, on the street, on a park bench, a corridor

---

[37] Rao, Maya (2020) *Watch that Train, Watch that Girl*. www.youtube.com/watch?v=h3w89Jr Ho3Q&t=366s.

[38] Some of the activists have been released on bail. These include Natasha Narwal and Devangana Kalita, who lead a feminist students' group fighting for the rights of young women. The group is called Pinjra Tod (Bird in a Cage); its activism involves protest songs and street plays (see Paridhi Gupta, 2018).

[39] Rao, Maya (2021), *Can't Breathe, Will Speak* (circulated on WhatsApp on 6 May 2021).

I will speak, I may not breathe –
Let them free:
Sudha Bharadwaj, Shoma Sen, Devangana Kalita, Stan Swamy,
  Gautam Navlakha, Ronnie Wilson, Umar Khalid, Natasha
  Narewal (a refrain comes in) so many more . . . Jyoti Raghoba
  Jagtap, Safoora Zargar, Gulfisha Fathima, Ishrat Jahan . . . so
  many more . . .
They have names – everyday in the streets, corridors, in a van
Not yet outside your gate.
The real virus step aside,
Verdict? Did you say genocide?

References

Allana, Amal (2021). Interview by Bishnupriya Dutt [Zoom], 22 June.

Arora, Swati (2019a). Walking at Midnight: Women and Danger on Delhi's Streets, Walking in/as Publics. *Journal of Public Pedagogies*, 4, 171–6.

(2019b). Be a Little Careful: Women, Violence and Performance in India. *New Theatre Quarterly*, 35(1), 3–18.

(2020). *Walk* in India and South Africa: Notes towards a Decolonial and Transnational Feminist Politics. *South African Theatre Journal*, 32(2), 14–33.

Aston, Elaine, and Harris, Geraldine (eds.) (2007). *Feminist Futures?* London: Palgrave Macmillan.

Aston, Elaine, and Harris, Geraldine (2013). *A Good Night Out for the Girls: Popular Feminisms in Contemporary Theatre and Performance*. London: Palgrave Macmillan.

Balme, Christopher (2014). *The Theatrical Public Sphere*. Cambridge: Cambridge University Press.

Baxi, Pratiksha (2014). *Public Secrets of Law: Rape Trials in India*. Delhi: Oxford University Press.

Butler, Judith (2015). *Notes towards a Performative Theory of Assembly*. Cambridge, MA: Harvard University Press.

Chakravarti, Uma (2012). Cultures of Resistance: The Women's Movement As Performance. In Kavita Panjabi and Paromita Chakravarti, eds., *Women Contesting Culture*. Kolkata: Stree, Jadavpur University, pp. 58–71.

Chatterjee, Partha (2016). Theatre and the Publics of Democracy: Between Melodrama and Rational Realism. *Theatre Research International*, 41(3), 202–17. https://doi.org/10.1017/S0307883316000419

Chaudhuri, Amit (2020). Reclaiming the Republic. *Indian Express*, 25 January, p. 15, columns 1–4.

Dean, Jodi (2018). *Crowds and Party*. London: Verso.

Diamond, Elin (1997). *Unmaking Mimesis: Essays on Feminism and Theatre*. New York: Routledge.

Durham, Meenakshi Gigi (2014). Scene of the Crime: News Discourse of Rape in India and the Geopolitics of Sexual Assault. *Feminist Media Studies*, 15(2), 175–91. https://doi.org/10.1080/14680777.2014.930061

Dutt, Bishnupriya (2015). Performing Resistance with Maya Rao: Trauma and Protest in India. *Contemporary Theatre Review*, 25(3), 371–86.

(2017). Protesting Violence: Feminist Performance Activism in Contemporary India. In Elin Diamond, Denise Varnay, and Candice Amich, eds., *Performance, Feminism and Affect in Neo-liberal Times*. London: Palgrave Macmillan, pp. 105–16.

Fisher, Tony (Forthcoming 2023). 'Taxonomy of the Political Theatre'. in *The Aesthetic Exception: Essay on Art, Theatre and Politics*. (Manchester University Press).

Fisher, Tony, and Eve Katsouraki, eds. (2017). *Performing Antagonism: Theatre, Performance and Radical Democracy*. London: Palgrave Macmillan.

Ghosh, Priyam (2014). Performing Protest: Feminist/Queer Sexuality in Public Spaces 2009 Onwards. Unpublished M.Phil. thesis, Jawaharlal Nehru University, Delhi.

Gluhovic, Milija (2020). *Theories of Theatre, Memories*. London: Bloomsbury.

Goswami, Sohini (2021). Farm Laws Stir: All-Women Brigade Holds Kisan Sansad at Jantar Mantar Today. *Hindustan Times*, 26 July. www .hindustantimes.com/india-news/farm-laws-stir-all-women-brigade-holds-kisan-sansad-at-jantar-mantar-today-101627278225819.html

Griffin, Gabriele (2004). Troubling Identities: Clair Dowie's Why Is John Lennon Wearing a Skirt? In Maggie B. Gale and Viv Gardner, eds., *Auto/biography and Identity: Women, Theatre and Performance*. Manchester: Manchester University Press, pp. 153–77.

Gupta, Ankush (2012). Pink Nights: The Queer (Male) Discotheques of Delhi and Music As the Site of Performance. Unpublished M.Phil. thesis, Jawaharlal Nehru University, New Delhi.

Gupta, Paridhi (2018). Art(s) of Visibility: Resistance and Reclamation of University Spaces by Women Students in Delhi. *Gender Place & Culture*, 27(1), 86–101. https://doi.org/10.1080/0966369X.2019.1586652

Haksar, Anamika (2018). Theatre of Metaphor and Meaning. YouTube, 26 January. www.youtube.com/watch?v=EfCtWCdM0tY&t=2608s

India Today (2019). Pulwama Attack: Kashmiri Students from Various Parts of India Allege Harassment. C. R. P. F. Launches Helpline. 16 February. www .indiatoday.in/india/story/pulwama-terror-attack-kashmiri-students-allege-harassment-crpf-helpline-1457910-2019-02-16

Indian Express (2019). Will Take Fight against Terror into Its Home. 5 March.

Jayal, Niraja Gopal (2019). Faith Based Citizenship: The Dangerous Path India Is Choosing. *India Forum*, 13 November. www.theindiaforum.in/article/ faith-criterion-citizenship

Jestrovic, Silvija (2020). *Performances of Authorial Presence and Absence: The Author Dies Hard*. London: Palgrave Macmillan.

John, Mary E. (ed.) (2008). Introduction. In *Women's Studies in India: A Reader*. Delhi: Penguin Books, pp. 1–22.

Joseph, Sarah (2007). Neoliberal Reforms and Democracy in India. *Economic and Political Weekly* 42(31). www.epw.in/journal/2007/31/perspectives/neoliberal-reforms-and-democracy-india.html

Kapur, Anuradha (2009). Reassembling the Modern: An Indian Theatre Map since Independence. In Nandi Bhatia, ed., *Modern Indian Theatre: A Reader*. Delhi: Oxford University Press, pp. 31–40.

(2021a). Interview by Bishnupriya Dutt [Zoom], 10 April.

(2021b). Interview by Bishnupriya Dutt [Zoom], 15 June.

Kishwar, Madhu, and Vanita, Ruth (2008). Initiatives against Dowry Deaths. In Mary E. John, ed., *Women's Studies in India: A Reader*. Delhi: Penguin Books, pp. 42–5.

Kumar, Radha (2011). *The History of Doing*. Delhi: Zubaan.

Lieder, Frances K. (2015). Not-Feminism: A Discourse on the Politics of a Term in Modern Indian Theatre. *Asian Theatre Journal* 32(2), 598–618. https://doi.org/10.1353/atj.2015.0053

Mangai, A. (2015). *Acting Up: Gender and Theatre in India*. Delhi: Leftword.

Menon, Nivedita (2011). *Recovering Subversion: Feminist Politics beyond Law*. 2nd ed. Delhi: Permanent Black.

Menon, Nivedita, ed. (2012). Introduction. In *Gender and Politics in India*. Delhi: Oxford University Press, pp. 1–36.

Narayanan, Mundoli (2010). The Politics of Memory: The Rise of the Anti-hero in Kathakali. In Pallabi Chakravarti and Nilanjana Gupta, eds., *Dance Matters: Performing India on Local and Global Stages*. New York: Routledge, pp. 237–64.

Om Swaha, Nukkad, Nukkad, Angan, Angan (1988). Delhi: Jagori Collective, pp. 42–51.

Parameswaran, Ameet (2016). Performance, Protest, and the Intimate Public. *The Drama Review*, 60(2), 2–3.

Patil, Vrushali, and Purkayastha, Bandana (2018). The Transnational Assemblage of Indian Rape Culture. *Ethnic and Racial Studies*, 41(11), 1952–70. https://doi.org/10.1080/01419870.2017.1322707

Rai, Shirin M., and Reinelt, Janelle (eds.) (2015). *The Grammar of Politics and Performance*. London: Routledge.

Rao, Maya (2020). Theatre and the Political in the Age of Global Pandemic. *Cultures of the Left*. YouTube. 15 June. www.youtube.com/watch?v=KxJLiigb6s8

(2021a). Correspondence around *Lady Macbeth at Home* and *Lady Macbeth Revisited*. August.

(2021b). Correspondence with Maya Rao. December.

(2021c). Group discussion with members of the Theatre Union organized by Natrang Pratishthan as part of a lecture series titled Rang Smaran. 19 March. https://warwick.ac.uk/fac/arts/scapvc/theatre/research/current/culturesoftheleft/newsandevents.

(2021d). Interview by Bishnupriya Dutt [Zoom]. 12 April.

(2021e). Interview as part of an international online teaching programme, IVAC-DAAD workshop, a collaboration between Jawaharlal Nehru University, University of Cologne, and Theatre School, Pontificia Universidad Católica de Chile. 9 July.

Ray, Raka (2000). *Fields of Protest: Women's Movement in India*. Delhi: Kali for Women.

Reinelt, Janelle (1996). Beyond Brecht: Britain's New Feminist Drama. In Helene Keyssar, ed., *Feminist Theatre and Theory*. New York: St. Martin's Press.

(2012). Keynote lecture given in Belgrade, Serbia, 8 November, on the occasion of the publication of Reinelt's *Politics and Performance: Collected Essays* (*Politika Iizvođačke Umetnosti: Zbirka eseja*). Milija Gluhovic and Ivana Vujić, eds., and Smiljka Kesić, Željiko Maksimović, Marija Pavlović, Vesna Sofrenović, Aneta Stojnič, and Milica Šešić, trans. Belgrade: University of Belgrade Press.

Richmond, Farley P., Swann, Darius L., and Zarilli, Philipp B. (1983). *Indian Theatre: Traditions of Performance*. Delhi: Motilal Banarasidass.

Roy, Anupama (2014). Critical Events, Incremental Memories and Gendered Violence. *Australian Feminist Studies*, 29(81), 238–54. https://doi.org/10.1080/08164649.2014.959161

(2016). *Citizenship in India*. Delhi: Oxford University Press.

Salam, Zuya Us, and Ausaf, Uzma (2020). Shaheen Bagh: *From a Protest to a Movement*. Delhi: Bloomsbury.

Sangari, Kumkum (2012). Gendered Violence, National Boundaries and Culture. In Kavita Panjabi and Paromita Chakravarti, eds., *Women Contesting Culture*. Kolkata: Stree, Jadavpur University, pp. 324–43.

Schechner, Richard (2004). *Performance Theory*. New York: Routledge.

Sen, Samita (2003). Towards a Feminist Politics? The Indian Women's Movement in historical Perspective. In Karin Kapadia, ed., *The Violence of Development*. Delhi: Zubaan.

Shalson, Lara (2017). *Theatre and Protest*. London: Palgrave.

(2018). *Performing Endurance: Art and Politics since 1960*. Cambridge: Cambridge University Press.

Shakespeare, William (2014). *The Complete Works of William Shakespeare.* San Diego: Cantebury Classics.

Shrangi, Vatsala (2020). As migrant workers return home, lack of workforce hits businesses in Delhi. *Hindustan Times*, 2 Jun. www.hindustantimes.com/delhi-news/as-migrant-workers-return-home-lack-of-workforce-hits-businesses-in-delhi/story-5I90E2zIUOSiWkpvIQaq6M.html.

Sen, Samita (2003). Towards a Feminist Politics? The Indian Women's Movement in Historical Perspective. In Karin Kapadia, ed., *The Violence of Development*, Delhi: Zubaan.

Zarilli, Philip B. (1984). *The Kathakali Complex.* Delhi: Abhinav.

    (2000). *Kathakali Dance Drama: Where Gods and Demons Come to Play.* London: Routledge.

Acknowledgements

This Element is an attempt to demonstrate my deep admiration for the feminist activists, performers, and performance makers, Maya Rao and her collaborators, Amal Allana, Anamika Haksar, Anuradha Kapur, and many others who have created and continue to contribute to vibrant feminist-theatre practices.

I am grateful to my friends and colleagues for their generosity and support, and to my students at the School of Arts and Aesthetics, JNU, who, over the years, through their coursework and research, have engaged with my interest in feminist theatre. I specially thank Anuradha Kapur, Silvija Jestrovic, Ameet Parameswaran, and Mallarika Sinha Roy, who read through and advised on drafts; Abhilash Pillai for magnanimously providing me with videos, photographs, and resources; and Semanti Basu for working with me on the manuscript through the isolation of the lockdown. Janelle Reinelt has always been my role model, and her intellectual generosity is what I aspire to.

I am also indebted to the many conversations on feminist practices in India that arose over the years through the International Federation for Theatre Research's Feminist Research Working Group, and JNU's collaboration with the University of Warwick. I specially want to mention Sue Ellen Case, who many years ago urged me to work on Maya Krishna Rao; Elaine Aston, who invited me to write about her and collaborated in a true feminist mode; and Elin Diamond, Milija Gluhovic, and Denise Varney, who were always eager to read my papers and ask pertinent questions.

My family has always seen politics and art as an integral aspect of life. I miss Noel's constant distraction tactics, trying to get attention while I work. Thanks to Debashis for his steadfast support and to the feisty feminist in my family, Ahvana, I owe my inspiration and commitment to feminist practices and the struggles ahead.

Cambridge Elements ☰

Women Theatre Makers

Elaine Aston
Lancaster University
Elaine Aston is internationally acclaimed for her feminism and theatre research.
Her monographs include *Caryl Churchill* (1997), *Feminism and Theatre* (1995), *Feminist Theatre Practice* (1999), *Feminist Views on the English Stage* (2003), and *Restaging Feminisms* (2020). She has served as Senior Editor of *Theatre Research International* (2010–12) and President of the International Federation for Theatre Research (2019–23).

Melissa Sihra
Trinity College Dublin
Melissa Sihra is Associate Professor in Drama and Theatre Studies at Trinity College Dublin.
She is author of *Marina Carr: Pastures of the Unknown* (2018) and editor of *Women in Irish Drama: A Century of Authorship and Representation* (2007). She was President of the Irish Society for Theatre Research (2011–15) and is currently researching a feminist historiography of the Irish playwright and co-founder of the Abbey Theatre, Lady Augusta Gregory.

Advisory Board
Nobuko Anan, *Kansai University, Japan*
Awo Mana Asiedu, *University of Ghana*
Ana Bernstein, *UNIRIO, Brazil*
Elin Diamond, *Rutgers, USA*
Bishnupriya Dutt, *JNU, India*
Penny Farfan, *University of Calgary, Canada*
Lesley Ferris, *Ohio State University, USA*
Lisa FitzPatrick, *University of Ulster, Northern Ireland*
Lynette Goddard, *Royal Holloway, University of London, UK*
Sarah Gorman, *Roehampton University, UK*
Aoife Monks, *Queen Mary, London University, UK*
Kim Solga, *Western University, Canada*
Denise Varney, *University of Melbourne, Australia*

About the Series
This innovative, inclusive series showcases women-identifying theatre makers from around the world. Expansive in chronological and geographical scope, the series encompasses practitioners from the late nineteenth century onwards and addresses a global, comprehensive range of creatives – from playwrights and performers to directors and designers.

Printed in the United States
by Baker & Taylor Publisher Services